Scott Foresman

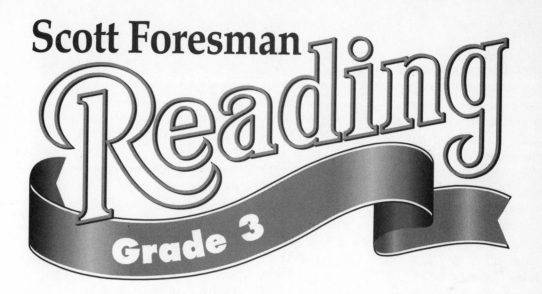

Reading
Grade 3

Phonics
Workbook

Scott Foresman

Editorial Offices: Glenview, Illinois • New York, New York
Sales Offices: Reading, Massachusetts • Duluth, Georgia • Glenview, Illinois
Carrollton, Texas • Menlo Park, California

Editorial Offices: Glenview, Illinois • New York, New York
Sales Offices: Reading, Massachusetts • Duluth, Georgia • Glenview, Illinois
Carrollton, Texas • Menlo Park, California

ISBN 0-673-61427-1

910-CRK-0605040302

© Scott Foresman 3

Name **Mrs. Swift**

The letter *a* stands for the short *a* vowel sound in *cat*.
The letter *e* stands for the short *e* vowel sound in *net*.
The letter *i* stands for the short *i* vowel sound in *hit*.

Say each picture name. Write the letter that stands for the vowel sound.

1.  e _____

2.  i _____

3.  e _____

4.  a _____

5.  a _____

6. i _____

7.  a _____

8.  i _____

9.  i _____

10.  e _____

 Notes for Home: Your child identified the short vowel sounds *a*, *e*, and *i* in picture names.
Home Activity: Together with your child find objects in the room whose names have short vowel sounds. Tell what short vowel sound you hear in each object's name.

The letter *o* stands for the short *o* vowel sound in *hot*.
The letter *u* stands for the short *u* vowel sound in *luck*.

Underline the words with the same vowel sound as the first word in the row. Then follow the directions.

hot   **1.**   clock   rose   roll   rock

       2.   Write two words that rhyme with *hot.*

_____ _____ _____

run   **3.**   sum   cute   turn   must

       4.   Write two words that rhyme with *run.*

_____ _____

mug   **5.**   count   cut   cup   cube

       6.   Write two words that rhyme with *mug.*

_____ _____

not   **7.**   hold   knob   load   stop

       8.   Write two words that rhyme with *not.*

_____ _____

lock   **9.**   top   pond   bowl   stove

       10.   Write two words that rhyme with *lock.*

_____ _____

Notes for Home: Your child identified words with the short vowel sounds *o* and *u*.
Home Activity: Have your child make up sentences using the words in dark type.

2

Name _Nicole_

The letters *a, e, i, o,* and *u* stand for the short vowel sounds in words.

    cat   **net**   **hit**   **hot**   **luck**

Underline two words that have the same short vowel sound as the word at the beginning of the row.

lame-o!

1. trick	lion	quit	shirt	gift
2. spent	next	center	deep	knee
3. stamp	game	salt	stand	after
4. rock	job	home	note	stop
5. just	fur	music	summer	sudden
6. fast	table	band	ask	wait
7. left	each	sleep	empty	set
8. fun	number	excuse	study	fuel
9. cot	coin	enjoy	clock	cannot
10. inch	bike	this	until	time

Notes for Home: Your child identified words with short vowel sounds. **Home Activity:** Have your child choose a favorite book and name words from that book that have short vowel sounds.

Name_____

Sometimes the spelling of a base word changes when *-ed* is added.

jump—jump**ed**   no change
clap—clap**ped**   double the final
                          consonant

chase—cha**sed**   drop the final *e*
try—tr**ied**   change *y* to *i*

Write each *-ed* word under the heading that tells what happened to the base word when *-ed* was added.

~~slipped~~   ~~relaxed~~   ~~captured~~   ~~worried~~   ~~shared~~
~~carried~~   ~~stopped~~   ~~played~~   ~~discovered~~   ~~studied~~

No Change

1. relaxed

2. slipped

3. carried

Dropped the Final *e*

4. captured

5. played

Doubled the Final Consonant

6. stopped

7. discovery

Changed *y* to *i*

8. worried

9. shared

10. studied

Name _____

Sometimes the spelling of a base word changes when -*ing* is added.

jump—jump**ing**   no change
smile—smil**ing**   drop the final *e*
hop—hop**ping**   double the final consonant

Add -*ing* to each word. Write the new word on the line.

1. charge ___charging___   2. win ___wining___

3. recite ___reciting___   4. discover ___discovering___

5. get ___getting___   6. circle ___circling___

7. visit ___visiting___   8. strum ___struming___

9. ride ___riding___   10. sing ___singing___

Write the word from above that completes each sentence.

11. On my summer vacation, I will be ___visiting___ a ranch.

12. I will be ___getting___ a new pair of cowboy boots for the trip.

13. Each day I will go ___riding___ on a horse.

14. Maybe I will even try ___struming___ a guitar.

15. I will be ___discovering___ many new things.

Notes for Home: Your child added the -*ing* ending to words. **Home Activity:** Take turns with your child telling a story about a family trip you would like to take. Use words ending in -*ing*.

Name_____

Some words have double consonants in the middle: *butter, dinner*. The two consonants stand for one sound.

Underline the words with double consonants in the middle.

1. little	**2.** follow	**3.** pepper	**4.** double	**5.** different
6. sorry	**7.** three	**8.** batter	**9.** tomorrow	**10.** kitchen
11. pretty	**12.** forest	**13.** wheel	**14.** happy	**15.** summer

Write the opposite of each word. Use a word from the box.

16. same _____

17. salt _____

18. pitcher _____

19. lead _____

20. glad _____

21. ugly _____

22. big _____

23. sad _____

24. today _____

25. winter _____

Notes for Home: Your child identified words with double consonants in the middle.
Home Activity: Have your child choose a word he or she wrote and give another word that has a similar meaning.

Name **Nicole**

Some words have double consonants at the end: *still, gruff*. The two consonants stand for one sound.

Write the two letters that stand for the ending sound in each picture name.

1.  *ss*

2.  *ll*

3.  *gg*

4.  *ss*

5.  *ll*

6. 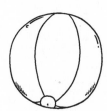 *tt*

7.  *ff*

8.  *ll*

9.  *ll*

10.  *ss*

 Notes for Home: Your child identified words with double consonants at the end.
Home Activity: Have your child look through a magazine and find other words that have double consonants at the end.

The *a*-consonant-*e* pattern stands for the long *a* vowel sound.

bake   same

Underline each word with the long *a* sound spelled *a*-consonant-*e*. Then use the underlined words to complete the story.

1. made   2. day   3. fame   4. safe

5. way   6. name   7. paid   8. take

9. came   10. trail   11. pale   12. ate

13. Goldilocks is a girl's __name__.

14. She gained __fame__ in a story about three bears.

15. One day she __came__ to a house in the woods.

16. She __ate__ some of the bears' porridge.

17. Goldilocks __made__ herself comfortable by sitting in their chairs.

18. Then she tried to __take__ a nap.

19. When she saw the bears, she turned __pale__.

20. She ran from the house until she was __safe__.

Notes for Home: Your child wrote words with the long *a* vowel sound spelled *a*-consonant-*e*. **Home Activity:** Take turns with your child telling a favorite story. Listen for words with the long *a* sound and name them.

The *i*-consonant-*e* pattern stands for the long *i* vowel sound.

        nice   **fine**

Draw a line from each picture to the word for the picture.

easy

1.

dine
dim
(dime)

2.

fine
(five)
fire

3.

ride
(rice)
ripe

4.

pile
(pine)
pin

5.

prize
prime
(price)

6.

Mike
mile
(mice)

7.

(bike)
bide
bite

8.

(kite)
kind
kite

9.

hire
hike
(hive)

10.

(line)
life
lime

Notes for Home: Your child identified words with the long *i* vowel sound spelled
i-consonant-*e*. **Home Activity:** Take turns with your child choosing a long *i* word from the
page and making up a silly sentence for the word.

Name _____

The *o*-consonant-*e* pattern stands for the long *o* vowel sound.

woke   **hope**

Write the word that answers each clue and has the long *o* sound spelled
o-consonant-*e*.

1. something to wear to keep warm
   robe   coat   _____

2. a place to live
   house   home   _____

3. a holder for ice cream
   cone   carton   _____

4. something a cowhand uses
   rope   road   _____

5. a beautiful flower
   rose   daffodil   _____

6. a place to cook
   stove   pot   _____

7. something you might break if you fall
   bone   toe   _____

8. where electric wires might be hung
   post   pole   _____

9. a part of your face
   eyebrows   nose   _____

10. a way to look at the stars
    window   telescope   _____

Notes for Home: Your child wrote words with the long *o* vowel sound spelled
o-consonant-*e*. **Home Activity:** With your child, make up meaning clues for these long *o*
words: *stone, vote, globe, hose.*

The long *e* sound can be spelled *ee, ea, ie,* and *ey.*

te**ee**th   t**ea**ch   sh**ie**ld   donk**ey**

Follow the directions in each sentence. Choose words from the box.

> movie   reach   cookie   monkey   sweet   feet   beach

1. Write two words that rhyme with *peach.*

_____   _____

2. Circle the way long *e* is spelled in the words you wrote.   ee   ea   ie   ey

3. Change the first letter of *donkey.* Write a word from the box.

_____

4. Circle the way long *e* is spelled in the word you wrote.   ee   ea   ie   ey

5. Write a word for a treat to eat with milk. _____

6. Circle the way long *e* is spelled in the word you wrote.   ee   ea   ie   ey

7. Write two words that rhyme with *meet.*

_____   _____

8. Circle the way long *e* is spelled in the words you wrote.   ee   ea   ie   ey

9. Write a word for what you see on a video.

_____

10. Circle the way long *e* is spelled in the word you wrote.   ee   ea   ie   ey

Notes for Home: Your child wrote words with different spellings for the long *e* sound.
Home Activity: Look through a newspaper together to find words with long *e* spelled *ee, ea, ie,* or *ey.* Circle the words as you find them.

Name _____

The long *e* sound can be spelled *y* or *e*.

busy   me

Underline the words with the long *e* sound spelled *y*. Circle the words with the long *e* sound spelled *e*.

1. excitedly   **2.** she   **3.** zebra

4. buggy   **5.** ugly   **6.** we

7. funny   **8.** maybe   **9.** everybody

Read each sentence. Change the underlined word or words to a word from above. Write the word.

10. Jake had a dog that was <u>not pretty</u>.

11. Everyone thought Jake's dog, Muttsy, was <u>odd</u> looking.

_____   _____

12. When people laughed at her, <u>Muttsy</u> would bark at them.

13. One day Muttsy showed <u>all Jake's friends</u> what a good dog she was.

_____   _____

14. Muttsy kept a baby <u>carriage</u> from rolling into the street.

15. Then all the people cheered <u>frantically</u>.

_____   _____

Notes for Home: Your child wrote words in which the long *e* sound is spelled *y* and *e*.
Home Activity: Together with your child tell a story about a dog. Use some of the long *e* words from the page.

The long *e* sound can be spelled in many different ways.

ee	as in	**f**ee**t**	**ey**	as in	vall**ey**
ea	as in	s**ea**t	**y**	as in	an**y**
ie	as in	**f**ie**ld**	**e**	as in	w**e**

Follow the long *e* path. In each box, underline two words with the long *e* sound. Circle the letter or letters that stand for the sound.

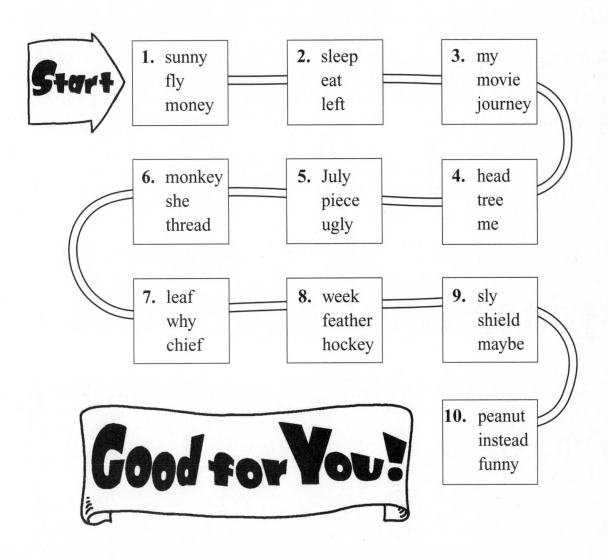

1. sunny
   fly
   money

2. sleep
   eat
   left

3. my
   movie
   journey

6. monkey
   she
   thread

5. July
   piece
   ugly

4. head
   tree
   me

7. leaf
   why
   chief

8. week
   feather
   hockey

9. sly
   shield
   maybe

10. peanut
    instead
    funny

Good for You!

Notes for Home: Your child identified words with different spellings for the long *e* sound. **Home Activity:** Ask your child think of another long *e* word for each pattern—*ee, ea, ie, ey, y,* and *e.*

Double consonants may come in the middle or at the end of words. The two letters usually stand for one sound.

ki**tt**en   mi**rr**or   stu**ff**   se**ll**

Underline the word that completes each sentence and has double consonants.

1. Each morning you must ___.   eat   dress   wash

2. At the beach you might pick up a ___.   shell   crab   fish

3. An iron is used to ___ clothes.   wrinkle   heat   press

4. When writing, be sure to ___ correctly.   write   print   spell

5. One cent is also called a ___.   penny   coin   dollar

6. If something is small, it might be called ___.   wee   tiny   little

7. A special kind of church is called a ___.   place   mission   building

8. A thief is also called a ___.   burglar   robber   crook

9. The sound a turkey makes is called a ___.   cheep   cluck   gobble

10. We had tacos for ___.   breakfast   lunch   dinner

Notes for Home: Your child identified words with double consonants in the middle or at the end. **Home Activity:** Have your child read the underlined words and write another sentence for each one.

© Scott Foresman 3

Name_____

Words may have double consonants in the middle as in the word *muffin* or at the end as in the word *still*. The two consonants stand for one sound.

Follow each set of directions. Use the words in the box.

scissors	pretty	sheriff	call	full
cliff	pillow	dollar	fuzz	little

Write two words that end like *bell*.

1. _____

2. _____

Write two words that have two *t*'s in the middle like *kitten*.

3. _____

4. _____

Write two words that have two *l*'s like the word *follow*.

5. _____

6. _____

Write two words that end like *stuff*.

7. _____

8. _____

Write another word with two *s*'s in the middle like the word *mission*.

9. _____

Write another word that ends like *jazz*.

10. _____

Notes for Home: Your child identified and wrote words with double consonants in the middle and at the end. **Home Activity:** With your child, look through a favorite book. Take turns pointing to and naming other words with double consonants.

Name_____

The letters _ai_ and _ay_ stand for the long _a_ vowel sound.

w**ai**t   d**ay**

Write each word in the box under the picture whose name has the same pattern for long _a_ as the word.

gray	drain	paid	trail	way
stay	braid	rain	play	snail
paint	today	may	train	hay

1. _____   9. _____

2. _____   10. _____

3. _____   11. _____

4. _____   12. _____

5. _____   13. _____

6. _____   14. _____

7. _____   15. _____

8. _____

Notes for Home: Your child wrote words in which the long _a_ sound is spelled _ai_ or _ay_.
Home Activity: Together use pairs of words from the box to make up rhymes.

Name_____

The letters *oa, ow,* and *o* stand for the long *o* sound.

b**oa**t   sh**ow**   g**o**

Write the letter or letters that stand for the long *o* sound in each word. Then use the words to complete the ads.

1. coat _____   **2.** bowl _____

3. gold _____   **4.** go _____

5. soap _____   **6.** groan _____

7. mow _____   **8.** auto _____

9. throat _____   **10.** snow _____

11.

12.

13.

14.

15.

 Notes for Home: Your child wrote words in which the long *o* sound is spelled *oa, ow,* or *o.*
Home Activity: With your child, look at some newspaper ads. Try to find words with long *o* spelled *oa, ow,* or *o.*

Name_____

The long *a* sound can be spelled *ai* and *ay*.   **rain**   **hay**

The long *o* sound can be spelled *oa, ow,* and *o*.   b**oa**t   sh**ow**   g**o**ld

Find the word in each sentence that has the long *a* or long *o* sound. Write the word and circle the letters that stand for the long *a* or long *o* vowel sound.

1. A long time ago there lived a prince.   _____

2. He had a pet goat called Rufus.   _____

3. Rufus liked to play in the queen's garden.   _____

4. He would sneak in and slowly eat all the flowers.   _____

5. The prince would groan when he saw what
Rufus had done.   _____

6. One day the prince had a plan.   _____

7. He could not wait to try his idea.   _____

8. So the prince led Rufus to the big front lawn.   _____

9. When Rufus saw all the dandelions, he
wiggled his tail happily.   _____

10. Now Rufus is the best lawn mower
for the palace.   _____

Notes for Home: Your child identified and wrote words with the long *a* and *o* vowel sounds.
Home Activity: With your child, tell another story about the prince and the goat. Use long *a*
and long *o* words.

Sheet, teacher, field, and *money* have the long *e* sound.

sheet   teacher   field   money

Write only the words and phrases that have the long *e* sound in the camping trip list.

money   sunscreen   peaches   meat

bread   pieces of rope   clean clothes   sweets

field glasses   matches   sweaters   donkeys

extra eggs   canteens   honey   thread

peanut butter   sleeping bags   handkerchiefs   cookies

Camping Trip List

1. _____

2. _____

3. _____

4. _____

5. _____

6. _____

7. _____

8. _____

9. _____

10. _____

11. _____

12. _____

13. _____

14. _____

15. _____

 Notes for Home: Your child identified and wrote words with the long *e* sound.
Home Activity: Together look at the things written on the list. Talk about what the campers might do with each thing.

The long *e* sound can be spelled *y* as in *hungry* or *e* as in *she.*

Underline the words in each box that have the long *e* sound. Then rewrite each sentence. Use a word from the box in place of the underlined word or words.

1. they	**2.** we	**3.** she	**4.** he

5. What did <u>Keesha</u> tell you about the party?

_____

6. <u>Dave and I</u> are planning to go early.

_____

7. reply	**8.** tasty	**9.** many
10. funny	**11.** windy	**12.** why

13. There were <u>lots of</u> people at the party.

_____

14. All the food was <u>good</u>.

_____

15. Jerry told <u>silly</u> stories.

_____

Notes for Home: Your child identified words with the long *e* sound. **Home Activity:** Talk with your child about a party that was fun. Name words with the long *e* sound that you use in your conversation.

© Scott Foresman 3

Name_____

The long *i* sound can be spelled *igh* and *y*.

migh**t**   m**y**

Write the answer to each clue and underline the letter or letters that stand for the long *i* sound.

light	sight	sky	tight	right
cry	thigh	reply	fry	fly

1. birds do this   _____

2. where to see stars   _____

3. one of the five senses   _____

4. the opposite of *left*   _____

5. babies do this when hungry   _____

6. a lamp will give you this   _____

7. to cook in oil   _____

8. part of your leg   _____

9. to answer a question   _____

10. the opposite of *loose*   _____

Notes for Home: Your child wrote words in which the long *i* sound is spelled *igh* or *y*.
Home Activity: Take turns with your child choosing a word from the list on the page and naming a rhyming word.

The long *u* sound can be spelled *u*-consonant-*e* or *u*.

fu**se**   **m**u**sic**

Write the word that belongs in each group of words. Then underline the pattern that spells the long *u* sound in the word.

January	united	huge	Utah	amuse
mule	cube	humorous	pupil	cute

1. March, July, December, _____   *u*-consonant-*e*   *u*

2. big, large, tremendous, _____   *u*-consonant-*e*   *u*

3. horse, zebra, donkey, _____   *u*-consonant-*e*   *u*

4. Illinois, Florida, Texas, _____   *u*-consonant-*e*   *u*

5. learner, scholar, student, _____   *u*-consonant-*e*   *u*

6. funny, silly, amusing, _____   *u*-consonant-*e*   *u*

7. rectangle, circle, pyramid, _____   *u*-consonant-*e*   *u*

8. delight, entertain, raise a smile, _____   *u*-consonant-*e*   *u*

9. cuddly, adorable, sweet, _____   *u*-consonant-*e*   *u*

10. joined, together, one, _____   *u*-consonant-*e*   *u*

 Notes for Home: Your child wrote words in which the long *u* sound is spelled *u*-consonant-*e* or *u*. **Home Activity:** Take turns with your child choosing a word he or she wrote on the page and giving a descriptive sentence for it.

Name_____

The long *i* sound can be spelled *igh* and *y*. **tigh**t by

The long *u* sound can be spelled *u*-consonant-*e* and *u*. **fuse** h**u**man

Write the words on the elephants in the correct lists.

cube mute
reply bright
night future
my amuse

cute menu
sky humor
sigh right
uniform

music fly
apply use
light

Long *i* Spelled *igh*

1. _____

2. _____

3. _____

4. _____

5. _____

Long *i* Spelled *y*

6. _____

7. _____

8. _____

9. _____

10. _____

Long *u* Spelled *u*-consonant-*e*

11. _____

12. _____

13. _____

14. _____

15. _____

Long *u* Spelled *u*

16. _____

17. _____

18. _____

19. _____

20. _____

Notes for Home: Your child wrote words with the long *i* and long *u* sounds.
Home Activity: Ask your child to add at least one more word to each list.

Name_____

The letters *a, e, i, o,* and *u* stand for short vowel sounds.

bat   bed   sit   hot   cut

Say each picture name. Write **Yes** if the word has a short vowel sound. Then write the letter that stands for the short vowel sound. Write **No** if the word does not have a short vowel sound.

1.
_____ _____

2.
_____ _____

3.
_____ _____

4.
_____ _____

5.
_____ _____

6.
_____ _____

7.
_____ _____

8.
_____ _____

9.
_____ _____

10.
_____ _____

Notes for Home: Your child identified words with short vowel sounds.
Home Activity: Have your child cut out magazine pictures whose names have short vowel sounds, paste the pictures on paper, and write the letters that stand for the short vowel sounds in the picture names.

Some words have short vowel sounds.

a	e	i	o	u
hat	ten	dish	hot	cup

Write the word that answers the question. Underline the letter that stands for the short vowel sound in the word.

1. If you were hot, would you use a jet, a mop, or a fan to get cool? _____

2. Does a mitt, a hand, or a lid cover a pot? _____

3. Would you wear a cap, a vest, or a muff on your head? _____

4. Would you ride on a bat, a bus, or a box? _____

5. What would you use to clean up a spill—a rug, a mitt, or a mop? _____

6. Would you see a sled, a shell, or a bib on a turtle? _____

7. Can a bat, a pig, or a pup fly? _____

8. Is a cat, a hen, or a fox a bird? _____

9. Would a cup, a cut, or a cot need a bandage? _____

10. Would you swim, run, or hop across a pond? _____

Notes for Home: Your child identified and wrote words with short vowel sounds.
Home Activity: Take turns with your child asking questions like those on the page. Use words with short vowel sounds as choices for the answers.

Name_____

A compound word is made up of two words.

air + plane = airplane

Draw lines to match words that make compound words. Write the compound words.

1. foot   coat   _____

2. rain   corn   _____

3. pop   ball   _____

4. hand   ring   _____

5. ear   stand   _____

6. bird   house   _____

7. gold   paper   _____

8. paint   stick   _____

9. drum   brush   _____

10. news   fish   _____

Notes for Home: Your child joined words to make and write compound words.
Home Activity: Write each small word on the page on a piece of scrap paper. Have your child match the papers to form compound words.

A compound word is made of two smaller words.

when + ever = whenever   left + over = leftover

Underline the compound word that completes the sentence. Then draw a line between the words that make up the compound word.

1. One spring morning after ___,   sunset
Mom called to me.   breakfast

2. She said we could plant some ___   raindrops
in the garden.   sunflowers

3. We went ___ into the backyard   outside
where we have a garden.   inside

4. ___ she turned over some dirt with   However
a shovel, I saw worms.   Whenever

5. ___ I had to pull up some big   Sometimes
clumps of weeds.   Anytime

6. Sparrows peeked out of the ___   bedroom
and watched us dig.   birdhouse

7. We knew that in time ___ beautiful   someone
would grow.   something

8. We sprinkled seeds on the soil, and then we pushed   into
the seeds ___ the soil with a rake.   onto

9. As a last step, we poured some ___   buttermilk
over the soil.   rainwater

10. In the ___, we spend a lot of time   wintertime
working in our garden.   summertime

Notes for Home: Your child identified the words that make up compound words.
Home Activity: Have your child continue the story by telling what happened after the sunflowers grew. Point out any compound words your child uses.

The letters *igh* and *y* stand for the long *i* sound in *tight* and *cry*.

Follow each direction.

1. Write **fly.** Circle the letter that spells the long *i* sound.   _____

2. Change **f** to **s.** Write the new word.   _____

3. Change **l** to **k.** Write the new word.   _____

4. Change **k** to **h.** Write the new word.   _____

5. Change **s** to **w.** Write the new word.   _____

---

6. Write **sigh.** Circle the letters that spell the long *i* sound.   _____

7. Add a **t** at the end. Write the new word.   _____

8. Change **s** to **t.** Write the new word.   _____

9. Change the first **t** to **n.** Write the new word.   _____

10. Add a **k** at the beginning. Write the new word.   _____

Notes for Home: Your child wrote words with the long *i* sound spelled *igh* or *y*.
Home Activity: Starting with the word *cry* or *light*, help your child change, add, or subtract letters to make new words.

Name_____

The long *u* sound can be spelled *u*-consonant-*e* or *u*.

cute   **u**nit

Denzel has to find all the words with long *u* spelled *u*-consonant-*e*. Maria has to find all the words with long *u* spelled *u*. Write the words in the correct lists. Not all the words will be used.

music	humor	use	future	mule
sum	amuse	pull	cube	cuteness
fuse	uniform	useful	menu	pupil
number	put	curl	push	burn
must	bush	human	huge	turtle

Denzel's List   **Maria's List**

1. _____   9. _____

2. _____   10. _____

3. _____   11. _____

4. _____   12. _____

5. _____   13. _____

6. _____   14. _____

7. _____   15. _____

8. _____

Notes for Home: Your child wrote words in which the long *u* sound is spelled *u*-consonant-*e* or *u*. **Home Activity:** Take turns with your child choosing a word from each list and making up an oral sentence for it.

The long *i* sound can be spelled *igh* and *y*.   **righ**t   **fly**

The long *u* sound can be spelled *u*-consonant-*e* and *u*.   **u**se   me**nu**

Write *i* or *u* to tell what long vowel sound you hear in each word. Then circle the pattern that spells the long vowel sound.

<u>Word</u>	<u>Vowel Sound Heard</u>	<u>How Is It Spelled?</u>			
1. mule	_____	*igh*	*y*	*u*-consonant-*e*	*u*
2. apply	_____	*igh*	*y*	*u*-consonant-*e*	*u*
3. high	_____	*igh*	*y*	*u*-consonant-*e*	*u*
4. flying	_____	*igh*	*y*	*u*-consonant-*e*	*u*
5. music	_____	*igh*	*y*	*u*-consonant-*e*	*u*
6. tighter	_____	*igh*	*y*	*u*-consonant-*e*	*u*
7. unit	_____	*igh*	*y*	*u*-consonant-*e*	*u*
8. cube	_____	*igh*	*y*	*u*-consonant-*e*	*u*
9. myself	_____	*igh*	*y*	*u*-consonant-*e*	*u*
10. amuse	_____	*igh*	*y*	*u*-consonant-*e*	*u*

Notes for Home: Your child identified the spelling patterns in long *i* and long *u* words.
Home Activity: Help your child list other long *i* and long *u* words. Ask your child what long vowel sound is heard in each word.

The letters *oo* stand for the vowel sounds in these words.

boo**t**   **g**oo**d**

Write each word under the word that has the same vowel sound.

book   foot   hoot   hood   zoo
moon   spoon   hook   broom   wood

soon   **look**

1. _____   6. _____

2. _____   7. _____

3. _____   8. _____

4. _____   9. _____

5. _____   10. _____

Write a word from above that answers each clue.

11. Eat soup with this.   _____

12. Catch fish on this.   _____

13. Owls do this.   _____

14. Sweep the floor with this.   _____

15. A jacket might have this.   _____

Notes for Home: Your child sorted words that have two vowel sounds spelled *oo*.
Home Activity: Have your child read the lists of words under *soon* and *look* and add more words to each list.

Name_____

The letters *oo* stand for the vowel sound in *look*.
The letters *oo* also stand for the vowel sound in *too*.

Unscramble the letters to make words from the list. Write the letters on the lines.
Underline the word at the right that has the same vowel sound as the word you made.

hook   fool   moon   boot   good

    wood   goose   hood   school

1. oogse   <u>1</u> __ __ __ __   look   cool

2. koco   <u>2</u> __ __ __   hook   zoo

3. ohod   <u>3</u> __ __ __   cookie   spool

4. tboo   <u>4</u> __ __ __   brook   loose

5. oodw   <u>5</u> __ __ __   took   noodle

6. cosolh   <u>6</u> __ __ __ __ __ __   shook   pool

7. borom   <u>7</u> __ __ __ __   wool   room

8. ogdo   <u>8</u> <u>9</u> __ __   book   noon

9. nomo   <u>10</u> __ __ __   stood   balloon

Write the numbered letters to answer the riddle.

Where is a place to learn?

10. __ __ __ __ __ __ __ __ __ __
    1   2   3   4   5   6   7   8   9   10

Notes for Home: Your child identified words with the *oo* vowel pattern.
Home Activity: List some other words with *oo*. Take turns with your child scrambling the words and having the other person write them correctly.

In *book*, the vowel sound is spelled *oo*.
In *noon*, the vowel sound is spelled *oo*.

Underline the word that has the same vowel sound as the picture name.

1. food   good

2. too   look

3. boot   wood

4. tool   hood

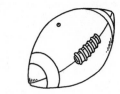

5. noon   good-bye

6. school   foot

7. cool   brook

8. soon   took

9. pool   stood

10. broom   cook

Notes for Home: Your child identified the vowel sounds in words with the *oo* pattern.
Home Activity: Have your child choose two words from the page and make up a silly
sentence for them.

A compound word is made from two smaller words.

　　　　back + yard = backyard　　　　　　any + body = anybody

Underline two words in each sentence that can be put together to make a compound word. Write the word.

1. I went up to the second floor using the stairs.　　_____

2. For a trip in space, you will need a ship.　　_____

3. He went out and played along the side of the house.　_____

4. She bought some toys but not another thing.　　_____

5. The air in the plane was hot and stuffy.　　_____

6. The bed in her room had not been made.　　_____

7. A bright moon gave us light to see by.　　_____

8. Did you see the sun as it set last evening?　　_____

9. There was a lot of news in today's paper.　　_____

10. Put the baby into the seat and fasten the belt.　　_____

Notes for Home: Your child combined words to make compound words.
Home Activity: Take turns with your child writing the first part of a compound word on a piece of paper and having the other person write the second part of the compound word.

A compound word is made up of two words put together.

in + to = into   any + body = anybody

Draw lines to match words to make compound words. Then write the compound words under the heading that tells about them.

1. foot	plane	**6.** rail	ground
2. out	ball	**7.** basket	ball
3. air	yard	**8.** play	ship
4. pop	side	**9.** space	berries
5. back	corn	**10.** straw	road

Sports

11. _____

12. _____

Food

13. _____

14. _____

Places

15. _____

16. _____

17. _____

Ways to Travel

18. _____

19. _____

20. _____

Notes for Home: Your child formed and classified compound words.
Home Activity: Together name other compound words. Think of a category name for each compound.

Name _____

The letters *ou* stand for the vowel sounds in these words.

| cloud | c**ou**ple | b**ou**lder | w**ou**ld | s**ou**p |

Write an *ou* word from the box that rhymes with the underlined word.

| double | you | ground | touch | group |
| house | should | shoulder | could | pounce |

1. See what I <u>found</u> lying on the _____.

2. Did you see a <u>mouse</u> in the basement of your _____?

3. I hope you made enough <u>soup</u> to feed the whole _____.

4. Each time the ball would <u>bounce</u>, the cat would _____.

5. If you water the plant too <u>much</u>, it will be too wet to _____.

6. If I had a saw, I _____ cut this great big piece of <u>wood</u>.

7. I cannot come to visit _____ because today I have the <u>flu</u>.

8. They moved the <u>boulder</u> off the road and onto the _____.

9. Whenever Dave is in <u>trouble</u>, he wishes he had a _____.

10. To keep my ears warm, I _____ pull up my jacket <u>hood</u>.

Notes for Home: Your child identified words with the *ou* vowel pattern.
Home Activity: Have your child look in a newspaper, find *ou* words, and name rhyming words.

Name_____

The letters *ou* stand for the vowel sounds in these words.

cl**ou**d   **tou**ch   b**ou**lder   w**ou**ld   y**ou**

Write each word in the box under the word that has the same vowel sound for *ou*.

should	young	could	shoulder	house
mouse	shout	country	soup	couple
double	group	loud	trouble	ground

ou as in *cloud*   **ou** as in *touch*

1. _____   6. _____

2. _____   7. _____

3. _____   8. _____

4. _____   9. _____

5. _____   10. _____

ou as in *would*   **ou** as in *you*

11. _____   13. _____

12. _____   14. _____

ou as in *boulder*

15. _____

Notes for Home: Your child grouped words according to their vowel sounds spelled *ou*.
Home Activity: Choose a word from the box and use it to begin a story. Ask your child to choose other words and use them to add to the story.

37

The letters *ou* stand for the vowel sounds in these words.

gr**ou**nd   sh**ou**ld   **you**   d**ou**ble   b**ou**lder

Write each word next to a word that has the same vowel sound.

---

about   you   could

1. would   _____

2. youth   _____

3. sound   _____

---

mouse   soup   poultry

4. ground   _____

5. shoulder   _____

6. toucan   _____

---

should   couple

7. young   _____

8. could   _____

---

trouble   cloud

9. about   _____

10. touch   _____

© Scott Foresman 3

Notes for Home: Your child wrote words with the *ou* vowel pattern.
Home Activity: Take turns with your child choosing two words from one of the boxes and making up a sentence with the two words.

The letters *oo* stand for the vowel sounds in *spoon* and *foot*.

Write each word in the box under the picture whose name has the same vowel sound as the word.

tooth	look	wood	moose	loop
hood	boot	moon	school	took
spool	cook	hook	book	stool
stood	shook	good	goose	zoo

1. _____

2. _____

3. _____

4. _____

5. _____

6. _____

7. _____

8. _____

9. _____

10. _____

11. _____

12. _____

13. _____

14. _____

15. _____

16. _____

17. _____

18. _____

19. _____

20. _____

Notes for Home: Your child sorted *oo* words according to their vowel sounds.
Home Activity: Take turns with your child scrambling words from the lists and writing them correctly.

The letters *oo* stand for the vowel sounds in *room* and *foot*.

Underline the words that have the same vowel sound as the word in dark type. Then write the underlined word that goes with each clue.

room

1. moon	**2.** boots	**3.** look	**4.** stood	**5.** school
6. shook	**7.** wood	**8.** shoots	**9.** tools	**10.** took

11. what cowhands wear on their feet _____

12. a hammer, saw, and wrench _____

13. something seen in the night sky _____

14. what a player does with a basketball _____

15. a place where children learn _____

took

16. choose	**17.** mood	**18.** foot	**19.** wood	**20.** loose
21. hook	**22.** soon	**23.** books	**24.** moose	**25.** hood

26. a place to hang a coat _____

27. what some furniture is made of _____

28. something on a jacket _____

29. something at the end of a leg _____

30. what you would see in a library _____

Notes for Home: Your child wrote words with the *oo* vowel pattern. **Home Activity:** Take turns with your child choosing a word from a list and naming words that rhyme with it.

The letter *j* stands for /j/ in *just*.
The letter *g* stands for /j/ in *gem*.

Underline the word in each sentence that has /j/. Circle the letter that spells /j/.

1. Did you read that page?   j   g

2. Giraffes have long necks.   j   g

3. A kangaroo can jump.   j   g

4. A jungle has many trees.   j   g

5. Do you enjoy singing?   j   g

6. Be gentle with pets.   j   g

7. Read about a giant in a story.   j   g

8. The first month is January.   j   g

9. Let's study about Jupiter.   j   g

10. They have a large cat.   j   g

Notes for Home: Your child identified words in which /j/ is spelled *j* or *g*.
Home Activity: Ask your child to make a sentence in which one word has /j/ spelled *j* or *g*.

The letter *s* stands for /s/ in *safe*.
The letter *c* stands for /s/ in *ice*.

Read each word. Circle **Yes** if you hear /s/. Circle **No** if you do not.

1. city

Yes   No

2. side

Yes   No

3. can

Yes   No

4. some

Yes   No

5. face

Yes   No

6. does

Yes   No

7. mice

Yes   No

8. call

Yes   No

9. once

Yes   No

10. please

Yes   No

11. center

Yes   No

12. bus

Yes   No

13. cent

Yes   No

14. summer

Yes   No

15. place

Yes   No

Notes for Home: Your child identified words with /s/ spelled *s* and *c*.
Home Activity: Work together to make your own game like the one on the page. Think of new words. Take turns circling Yes and No.

Name_____

The letters *j* and *g* can spell the *j* sound.   **jump**   **g**iant
The letters *s* and *c* can spell the *s* sound.   side   ri**c**e

Underline the words in the box that have /j/ spelled *j* or *g* or that have /s/ spelled *s* or *c*. Write the words you underline in ABC order.

1. joy	**2.** giraffe	**3.** page	**4.** goat	**5.** base
6. ice	**7.** cook	**8.** sent	**9.** gentle	**10.** jeep
11. was	**12.** race	**13.** cup	**14.** mice	**15.** gem
16. some	**17.** edge	**18.** cat	**19.** safe	**20.** city

ABC Order

21. _____   **29.** _____

22. _____   **30.** _____

23. _____   **31.** _____

24. _____   **32.** _____

25. _____   **33.** _____

26. _____   **34.** _____

27. _____   **35.** _____

28. _____

Notes for Home: Your child identified words in which *j* or *g* spelled /j/ and *s* or *c* spelled /s/.
Home Activity: Have your child choose three words with /j/ and /s/ from a book or magazine and write the words in ABC order.

The letters *ai* and *ay* can spell the long *a* sound.

h**ai**l   d**ay**

Write *ai* or *ay* to make the words in the list.

tray   mail   train   May
stay   brain   rain   away

1. r _____ _____ n   **2.** aw _____ _____

3. br _____ _____ n   **4.** tr _____ _____ n

5. st _____ _____   **6.** M _____ _____

7. m _____ _____ l   **8.** tr _____ _____

Write a word from above that answers each clue.

9. This is wet and falls in drops.   **10.** An engine and cars make up this.

_____   _____

11. If you do not leave, you do this.   **12.** This is the month after April.

_____   _____

13. A package might be called this.   **14.** You carry things on this.

_____   _____

15. You think with this.

_____

Notes for Home: Your child identified and wrote words with long *a* spelled *ai* and *ay*.
Home Activity: Have your child find and circle words in a newspaper in which long *a* is
spelled *ai* or *ay*.

© Scott Foresman 3

The letters *oa, ow,* and *o* stand for the long *o* sound.

bo*a*t   **sh*ow***   **m*o*st**

Put each sentence in the correct order. Circle two words with the long *o* sound.

1. The old is radio. _____

2. wore a coat one No. _____

3. this down Go road. _____

4. soap Does the float? _____

5. throat My is sore so. _____

6. coach is hero The a. _____

7. a toad a song Can croak? _____

8. is mowed The lawn almost.

_____

9. along the coast walked slowly We.

_____

10. poem The does not about snow rhyme.

_____

Notes for Home: Your child identified words with the long *o* sound spelled *oa, ow,* and *o.*
Home Activity: Have your child make up other sentences that have at least one word with the
long *o* sound.

The letters *ow* stand for the vowel sounds in these words.

                gr**ow**   h**ow**

Write words from the box to complete the phrases.

down	throw	window	now	town
snow	below	shower	slow	frown

1. not up, but _____

2. not door, but_____

3. not above, but _____

4. not catch, but _____

5. not later, but _____

6. not rain, but _____

7. not fast, but _____

8. not bath, but _____

9. not smile, but _____

10. not city, but _____

Write each word in the box under the word that has the same vowel sound.

                grow   **clown**

11. _____

16. _____

12. _____

17. _____

13. _____

18. _____

14. _____

19. _____

15. _____

20. _____

Notes for Home: Your child wrote words with the *ow* vowel pattern.
Home Activity: Take turns with your child naming a word on the page and then pointing to and naming another word on the page with the same vowel sound.

The letters *ow* stand for the vowel sounds in *grow* and *how*.

Write the word that goes with the picture. Circle the letters that stand for the vowel sound in *grow* or *how*.

clown	shower	crowd	crown	arrow
row	shadow	howl	crow	pillow

1.  _____

2.  _____

3. _____

4. _____

5.  _____

6. _____

7. _____

8.  _____

9.  _____

10. _____

Notes for Home: Your child identified and wrote words with the *ow* vowel pattern.
Home Activity: You and your child draw a picture of something whose name has the letters *ow*. Name each other's picture and then name another word with the same vowel sound.

Name_____

The letters *ow* stand for the vowel sounds in these words.

clown   below

Follow the directions. Write the new words. Then circle the answer to the question.

1. blow   Change **bl** to **gr**.   _____

Change **gr** to **cr**.   _____

Does *ow* stand for the same sound in each word you wrote?   Yes   No

2. row   Change **r** to **sn**.   _____

Change **sn** to **pl**.   _____

Does *ow* stand for the same sound in each word you wrote?   Yes   No

3. know   Change **kn** to **m**.   _____

Change **m** to **c**.   _____

Does *ow* stand for the same sound in each word you wrote?   Yes   No

4. power   Change **p** to **t**.   _____

Change **t** to **fl**.   _____

Does *ow* stand for the same sound in each word you wrote?   Yes   No

5. yellow   Change **ye** to **a**.   _____

Change **al** to **be**.   _____

Does *ow* stand for the same sound in each word you wrote?   Yes   No

Notes for Home: Your child wrote words with the *ow* vowel pattern.
Home Activity: Starting with *down, snow,* or *crown,* help your child change letters to make new words.

The letters *j* and *g* can stand for /j/.   **just**   **age**

In each category, write the words that have the *j* sound spelled *j* or *g*.

Months

January **1.** _____

June   **2.** _____

July   **3.** _____

August

Clothes

jacket **4.** _____

jumper **5.** _____

gloves **6.** _____

jeans

Size

huge   **7.** _____

big   **8.** _____

jumbo **9.** _____

large

Names

Ginger **10.** _____

Greg   **11.** _____

Joel   **12.** _____

George

Places

garden **13.** _____

Japan **14.** _____

region **15.** _____

village

Notes for Home: Your child wrote words in which /j/ is spelled *j* or *g*.
Home Activity: Take turns with your child naming another word that belongs in each group
and telling whether the word has /j/ spelled *j* or *g*.

The letters _s_ and _c_ can stand for /s/.   saw   race

Write the word that answers each clue. Circle the letter that stands for the _s_ sound.

| city | summer | mice | pencil | baseball |
| yes | sea | ceiling | cereal | soft |

1. the top of a room _____ s   c

2. a season of the year _____ s   c

3. place where many people live _____ s   c

4. the opposite of _no_ _____ s   c

5. something to write with _____ s   c

6. a large body of water _____ s   c

7. more than one mouse _____ s   c

8. something to eat in the morning _____ s   c

9. the opposite of _hard_ _____ s   c

10. a sport with a batter _____ s   c

© Scott Foresman 3

Notes for Home: Your child wrote words in which /s/ is spelled _s_ or _c_.
Home Activity: Ask your child to think of other words that have /s/ spelled _s_ or _c_ and to make up meaning clues for the words.

In some pairs of letters, only one letter stands for a sound. The other letter is silent. Note the silent letter in each of these words.

wrench   **kn**ob   fas**t**en   desi**gn**   cli**mb**

Write the letter that is not heard in each word.

1. wren _____   **2.** knot _____

3. knew _____   **4.** lamb _____

5. sign _____   **6.** wrap _____

7. wrong _____   **8.** assign _____

9. comb _____   **10.** listen _____

Write the word that completes each sentence. Use words from above.

11. Mary had a little _____.

12. She _____ it could not go to school with her.

13. It was _____ for her pet to follow her.

14. She read the _____ that said, "No pets at school!"

15. But the animal would not _____ to her and stay at home.

Notes for Home: Your child identified words with silent letters. **Home Activity:** Have your child read sentences on the page. Discuss how Mary could solve her problem.

Name_____

Each of these words has a silent letter—a letter that does not stand for a sound.

wrap   **kn**ot   fas**t**en   desi**gn**   com**b**

Write a rhyming word for each numbered word below.

write   sign   wreath   lamb   knuckle
knee   knit   thumb   reign   listen

1. fit _____

2. some _____

3. night _____

4. tree _____

5. mine _____

6. train _____

7. ham _____

8. buckle _____

9. teeth _____

10. glisten _____

Use the words you wrote above to answer these questions.

11. Which two words have a silent *w*?

_____   _____

12. Which three words have a silent *k*?

_____   _____   _____

13. Which word has a silent *t*? _____

14. Which two words have a silent *g*?

_____   _____

15. Which two words have a silent *b*?

_____   _____

Notes for Home: Your child identified silent letters in words. **Home Activity:** Have your child look through newspaper and magazine ads for other words with silent letters and then circle each word and tell what letter is silent.

Name_____

The letters *ou* stand for the vowel sounds in these words.

ground   sh**ou**ld   y**ou**   t**ou**ch   p**ou**ltry

Write each word on the line with the matching number. Then underline the word that rhymes with the word you wrote.

(5) soup   **(1)** double   **(9)** mouth   **(10)** shout   **(8)** shoulder
(2) boulder   **(4)** would   **(6)** cloud   **(3)** round   **(7)** pouch

1. _____   grouch   would   trouble

2. _____   shoulder   younger   prouder

3. _____   proud   pound   doubled

4. _____   sound   counted   could

5. _____   shout   bounce   group

6. _____   crowd   should   roughed

7. _____   though   young   couch

8. _____   boulder   counter   tougher

9. _____   fourth   south   count

10. _____   southern   about   thought

Notes for Home: Your child wrote words with the *ou* vowel pattern.
Home Activity: Take turns with your child choosing a word that was not underlined and giving a rhyming word.

53

Name_____

Listen to the different sounds the letters *ou* can stand for.

so**und**   **c**ou**ld**   **y**ou   **c**ou**ple**   **sh**ou**lder**

Put an X on the box if the letters *ou* stand for two different vowel sounds in the words.

1. about
   around   H
	2. should
	   would W
		3. toucan
		   scout G

4. double
   country   O
	5. proud
	   youth R
		6. you
		   soup A

7. mouth
   group   E
	8. touch
	   young F
		9. loud
		   noun I

10. house
   pound   R
	11. amount
	   trouble A
		12. poultry
		   boulder L

13. would
   found   T
	14. cougar
	   group H
		15. double
		   young D

Write the letters from the boxes with X's. There is a message for you.

____   ____   ____   ____   ____!

© Scott Foresman 3

Notes for Home: Your child identified words with the *ou* vowel pattern.
Home Activity: With your child, change one word in a box that has an X. Make both words have the same vowel sound for *ou*.

54

In each of these words, the letters *ou* stand for a different vowel sound.

ar**ou**nd   c**ou**ld   y**ou**   t**ou**ch   sh**ou**lder

Change the words to make new words with the *ou* vowel pattern. Add and subtract letters. Write each new word.

1. mouse – se + th =   _____

2. group – gr + s =   _____

3. should – ld + t =   _____

4. pouch – ch + nd =   _____

5. young – ng + th =   _____

6. couch – ch + ld =   _____

7. fountain – f + m =   _____

8. boulder – b + sh =   _____

9. toucan – an + h =   _____

10. could – ld + nt =   _____

Notes for Home: Your child wrote words with the *ou* vowel pattern.
Home Activity: Together write some words that have *ou* in them and make new words by subtracting and adding letters.

The letters *ar* and *or* stand for the vowel sounds in these words.

farm   **hor**n

Underline the word that has the same vowel sound as the picture name.

1.

cart   cord

2.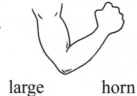

large   horn

3.

dark   orbit

4.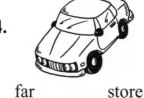

far   store

5.

farm   north

6.

card   story

7.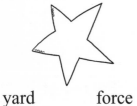

yard   force

8.

park   short

9.

bark   more

10.

part   fort

Notes for Home: Your child identified words with the *ar* and *or* vowel sounds.
Home Activity: Have your child look through magazines for pictures of things whose names have the *ar* or *or* vowel sound.

The letters *er, ir, or,* and *ur* stand for the vowel sound in these words.

he**r**	**b**i**r**d	**w**or**d	**f**ur

Write the word in the sentence that has the vowel sound in *her, bird, word,* and *fur.*
Circle the letters that stand for the vowel sound.

1. A fern is a plant. _____ er ir
    or ur

2. I have a burn on my hand. _____ er ir
    or ur

3. Turtles walk slowly. _____ er ir
    or ur

4. She won third prize. _____ er ir
    or ur

5. Draw a circle on the sidewalk. _____ er ir
    or ur

6. The poem has two verses. _____ er ir
    or ur

7. Here is a world map. _____ er ir
    or ur

8. I want to be a nurse. _____ er ir
    or ur

9. The skirt touched the ground. _____ er ir
    or ur

10. A worm is on the sidewalk. _____ er ir
    or ur

Notes for Home: Your child identified words with the *er, ir, or,* and *ur* vowel patterns.
Home Activity: Take turns with your child choosing a word written above. One person writes
the word, leaving out two letters. The other person guesses the word and writes the missing
letters.

Name _____

The letters *air* and *are* stand for the vowel sound in these words.　　**h**air**　**c**are**

The letters *ear* stand for the vowel sound in this word.　　**h**ear**

Write each word in the box that has a word with the same vowel sound and the same spelling.

pair	scare	clear	fear	hare
fair	dare	parent	flair	gear
near	air	dear	careful	stair

hair

1. _____

2. _____

3. _____

4. _____

5. _____

care

6. _____

7. _____

8. _____

9. _____

10. _____

hear

11. _____

12. _____

13. _____

14. _____

15. _____

Notes for Home: Your child identified words with the *air, are,* and *ear* vowel patterns.
Home Activity: Choose two words, each from a different box. Make up a sentence with them.
Then have your child take a turn doing the same thing.

Name_____

The letters *ow* stand for the vowel sounds in *own* and *down*.

Draw a line from the word in the box to the word with the same vowel sound.

1. now
grow
growl
own

2. owe
show
scowl
power

3. town
low
mow
brown

4. bowl
vowel
cow
owner

5. crow
crowd
tower
flow

6. shower
throw
now
snow

7. powder
plow
mower
blow

8. slow
own
frown
powder

9. tow
flower
how
glow

10. crown
allow
stow
below

Notes for Home: Your child matched words with the same vowel sound spelled *ow*.
Home Activity: With one hand, point to a word on the page. With the other hand, point to
another word with the same vowel sound. Then ask your child to take a turn.

Name _____

The letters *ow* stand for the vowel sounds in *down* and *own*.

Write a word from the box that has the same vowel sound as the underlined word and completes the sentence.

town	slowly	grow	bowling	mow
growling	vowel	throw	flower	towel

1. I <u>know</u> it is time for me to _____ the grass.

2. A large <u>crowd</u> gathered in the _____ square.

3. The <u>clown</u> had a _____ that squirted water.

4. I would like to <u>own</u> a red _____ ball.

5. The <u>snowman</u> _____ melted in the warm sun.

6. After my <u>shower</u>, I dried off with a _____.

7. The man <u>scowled</u> at the _____ dog.

8. Will you <u>show</u> me how to _____ a football?

9. The <u>row</u> of corn started to _____ tall.

10. <u>Somehow</u> I will learn all the _____ sounds.

Notes for Home: Your child wrote words with the *ow* vowel pattern.
Home Activity: Read two words from the box. Have your child tell if the two words have the same vowel sound. Then let your child read two words.

To find the base word, you must take off any prefixes, suffixes, or endings.

uncover   **care**ful   **search**es   re**build**ing

Add the prefixes, suffixes, or endings to the base words. Write the new word.

1. re + teach = _____

2. pull + ing = _____

3. re + fold + ed = _____

4. dis + honest + ly = _____

5. help + less + ness = _____

Write the base word for each word.

6. remake   **7.** played

_____   _____

8. dislike   **9.** unsafe

_____   _____

10. cheerful   **11.** stamping

_____   _____

12. unpacked   **13.** unfairness

_____   _____

14. incorrectly   **15.** replacement

_____   _____

© Scott Foresman 3

Notes for Home: Your child identified base words. **Home Activity:** Take turns with your child writing the words 6–15 as word equations like the examples in 1–5. Use plus and equal signs.

Sometimes the spelling of base words is changed when a suffix or ending is added.

The final *e* is dropped.	take	tak**ing**
The final consonant is doubled.	sit	sit**ting**
The final *y* is changed to *i*.	happy	happ**iness**

Write 1, 2, or 3 to show what happened to each base word. Then write the base word.

> **1.** The final *e* was dropped.
> **2.** The final consonant was doubled.
> **3.** The final *y* was changed to *i*.

1. stopped _____

2. riding _____

_____

_____

3. babies _____

4. waving _____

_____

_____

5. cutting _____

6. biggest _____

_____

_____

7. stories _____

8. hurried _____

_____

_____

9. approval _____

10. driver _____

_____

_____

Notes for Home: Your child identified the changes made to the spelling of base words when suffixes or endings were added. **Home Activity:** Using the base words that were written on the lines, help your child make up an adventure story.

Sometimes the spelling of a base word changes when a suffix or an ending is added.

Prefix Added

happy   **un**happy

Final Consonant Doubled

sit   sit**ting**

Final *e* Dropped

drive   driv**er**

Final *y* Changed to *i*

baby   bab**ies**

Write the base word of each word.

1. misplace   _____

2. bunnies   _____

3. gladness   _____

4. lovable   _____

5. hidden   _____

6. wiggling   _____

7. searches   _____

8. worried   _____

9. happily   _____

10. mysterious _____

Write the base word from above that completes each sentence.

11. Our _____ was missing.

12. How could he _____ out of the cage and escape?

13. We _____ him very much and want to find him.

14. Our pet makes us _____.

15. When we saw he was gone, we began to cry and _____.

16. "Let's _____ the yard," said Mother.

17. Our pet _____ himself very well.

18. When we found him, we were very _____.

19. We put him back in his _____ in the cage.

20. The _____ of the missing bunny was solved.

Notes for Home: Your child identified and wrote base words. **Home Activity:** Use the base words written for 1–10 to tell a story together about a family pet or adventure.

Name_____

The letters *ar, er, ir, or,* and *ur* stand for the vowel sounds in these words.

pa**rk**   **h**e**r**   **sk**i**rt**   **h**o**rn**   **b**u**rn**

Underline 15 words in the paragraph that have a vowel-*r* sound. Then write each word under the heading where it belongs.

When the dog began to bark, we knew something was wrong. Bert and I ran to the yard. We saw the dog digging up dirt by the porch. A large turtle was stuck between two slats. We were certain we could be of service. First we removed some soil in a circle around the animal. In a short time, it was free. It was not hurt, so we returned it to the pond. What a great story we had to tell!

ar as in *far*

1. _____

2. _____

3. _____

er as in *fern*

4. _____

5. _____

6. _____

ir as in *bird*

7. _____

8. _____

9. _____

or as in *fort*

10. _____

11. _____

12. _____

ur as in *turn*

13. _____

14. _____

15. _____

Notes for Home: Your child identified and sorted words with vowel-*r* sounds.
Home Activity: Tell a story about a time you helped someone. Then ask your child to tell a story about a time he or she helped someone.

The letters *air, are, ear,* and *or* stand for the vowel sounds in these words.

ch**air**   c**are**   d**ear**   w**or**d

Write the word from the box that goes with the meaning. Then circle the letters that stand for the vowel sound.

glare	clear	worst	hare	scare
near	world	pair	hear	hair

1. to frighten   _____

2. what covers your head   _____

3. two of a kind   _____

4. not cloudy   _____

5. an angry look   _____

6. another name for the Earth   _____

7. the opposite of *best*   _____

8. close to   _____

9. a kind of rabbit   _____

10. to listen to   _____

Notes for Home: Your child matched vowel-*r* words with meaning clues.
Home Activity: Make up a sentence for a word in the box. Have your child identify the word with the vowel-*r* sound. Continue until all the words are used.

A suffix is added to the end of a word.

dark + ness = dark**ness**   silent + ly = silent**ly**

arm + ful = arm**ful**   humor + ous = humor**ous**

Circle the suffix that can be added to the base word to make a new word. Then write the new word.

Word	Suffixes		New Word
1. care	ly	ful	_____
2. great	ness	ous	_____
3. final	ly	ous	_____
4. danger	ness	ous	_____
5. late	ly	ful	_____
6. joy	ous	ness	_____
7. kind	ness	ful	_____
8. near	ly	ous	_____
9. rest	ous	ful	_____
10. sad	ness	ful	_____
11. hope	ly	ful	_____
12. soft	ous	ness	_____
13. forget	ness	ful	_____
14. quick	ly	ous	_____
15. vigor	ous	ness	_____

Notes for Home: Your child added suffixes to base words to make new words.
Home Activity: Have your child find words with suffixes in newspaper ads and tell what suffix was added to each word.

When suffixes are added to words, they change the meaning of the words.

ness = a state of being ___   dark**ness** = a state of being dark

ly = in a ___ way   loud**ly** = in a loud way

ful = full of   hope**ful** = full of hope

ous = having ___   humor**ous** = having humor

Write the word for each meaning clue. Use the underlined word and one of these suffixes: *-ness, -ly, -ful, -ous.*

1. a state of being <u>quick</u>

_____

2. full of <u>hope</u>

_____

3. in a <u>soft</u> way

_____

4. having <u>joy</u>

_____

5. full of <u>power</u>

_____

6. in a <u>brave</u> way

_____

7. having <u>danger</u>

_____

8. a state of being <u>ill</u>

_____

9. a state of being <u>sad</u>

_____

10. full of <u>peace</u>

_____

11. in a <u>neat</u> way

_____

12. having <u>glamor</u>

_____

13. full of <u>use</u>

_____

14. a state of being <u>polite</u>

_____

15. in a <u>swift</u> way

_____

Notes for Home: Your child used meaning clues and suffixes to make new words.
Home Activity: Take turns with your child using words that were written on the page to make up sentences about famous people.

Sometimes the spelling of a base word changes before a suffix is added.

happy – y + i + ness = happiness

Add the suffix to each base word. Write the new word.

1. merry + ly = _____

2. mystery + ous = _____

3. happy + ly = _____

4. fury + ous = _____

5. crunchy + ness = _____

6. victory + ous = _____

7. empty + ness = _____

8. greedy + ness = _____

9. beauty + ful = _____

10. melody + ous = _____

11. easy + ly = _____

12. pretty + ness = _____

13. bumpy + ness = _____

14. angry + ly = _____

15. glory + ous = _____

Notes for Home: Your child changed the spelling of base words before adding suffixes.
Home Activity: Have your child add suffixes to the words *lazy, hungry,* and *busy* and tell how the spelling had to change.

Sometimes words have letters that do not stand for a sound.

write   **kn**ob   fas**t**en   **gn**at   lim**b**

Circle the word in each pair that has a silent consonant *w, k, t, g,* or *b.* Then write the word in the box where it belongs.

1. quarter   knot   **2.** fox   lamb

3. wrench   went   **4.** listen   hurt

5. kit   knee   **6.** germ   design

7. comb   cub   **8.** water   wreath

9. sign   hard   **10.** glisten   spot

silent *w*	**silent *k***
11. _____	13. _____
12. _____	14. _____
silent *t*	**silent *g***
15. _____	17. _____
16. _____	18. _____

silent *b*

19. _____

20. _____

Notes for Home: Your child identified and sorted words with silent letters.
Home Activity: Take turns with your child choosing a word, drawing a picture of it, and having the other person write the word for the picture.

Name_____

In some letter pairs, one letter is silent.

<u>wr</u>ite   <u>kn</u>ot   fas<u>t</u>en   <u>gn</u>at   crum<u>b</u>

Draw lines to match two words with the same silent letter. Then write each word pair and tell what letter is silent.

1. wrap	assign	6. comb	wreck
2. limb	glisten	7. resign	knock
3. sign	knit	8. listener	lamb
4. listen	climb	9. wren	design
5. knee	wreath	10. know	Christmas

11. The words _____ and _____ have a silent _____.

12. The words _____ and _____ have a silent _____.

13. The words _____ and _____ have a silent _____.

14. The words _____ and _____ have a silent _____.

15. The words _____ and _____ have a silent _____.

16. The words _____ and _____ have a silent _____.

17. The words _____ and _____ have a silent _____.

18. The words _____ and _____ have a silent _____.

19. The words _____ and _____ have a silent _____.

20. The words _____ and _____ have a silent _____.

Notes for Home: Your child identified silent letters in words. **Home Activity:** Take turns with your child making up a silly sentence for each pair of words and telling what letter is silent in the two words.

70

The letters *th, ch, ph,* and *sh* can sometimes be found in the middle of words. The two letters stand for one sound.

| fa**th**er | rea**ch**ed | telep**h**one | book**sh**elf |

Circle the letters that stand for the sound you hear in the middle of each picture name.

1.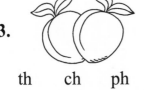

th   ch   ph   sh

2.

th   ch   ph   sh

3.

th   ch   ph   sh

4.

th   ch   ph   sh

5.

th   ch   ph   sh

6.

th   ch   ph   sh

7.

th   ch   ph   sh

8.

th   ch   ph   sh

9.

th   ch   ph   sh

10.

th   ch   ph   sh

Notes for Home: Your child identified consonant digraphs in the middle of words.
Home Activity: Have your child choose one of these consonant digraphs: *th, ch, ph, sh.* Together write all the words you can think of with these letters in the middle.

Name_____

The letters *th, ch, ph,* and *sh* can sometimes be found in the middle of words.

gather   reaches   telephone   fishing

Write the word from the box that answers each clue. Circle the letters *th, ch, ph,* or *sh* that appear in the middle of the word.

peaches	alphabet	trophy	seashells	perches
weather	elephant	beaches	father	bookshelves

1. This animal has a trunk.   _____

2. A dad may be called this.   _____

3. A beach is where these can be found.   _____

4. Rain, snow, and sun are part of this.   _____

5. You might win this as a prize.   _____

6. A library has many of these for books. _____

7. These feel fuzzy to the touch.   _____

8. These are sandy places.   _____

9. This is another name for the ABC's.   _____

10. These are places for birds to rest.   _____

Notes for Home: Your child wrote words with consonant digraphs in the middle.
Home Activity: Choose a word from the box and make up a clue for it. Ask your child to guess the word. Then have your child choose a word.

Sometimes the letters *th, ch, ph,* and *sh* stand for sounds heard in the middle of words.

anything   reaches   telephone   dashed

Write *th, ch, ph,* or *sh* to complete a word that makes sense in the sentence.

1. Look at that big gray ele___ ___ant.

2. I hope we have sun___ ___ine and not rain today.

3. Fill the ba___ ___tub with warm water.

4. Who coa___ ___es your team?

5. My grandfa___ ___er is coming for a visit.

6. Consuelo collects sea___ ___ells.

7. Did you buy any___ ___ing at the store?

8. My grades are un___ ___anged.

9. The first-prize winner received a tro___ ___y.

10. Do you know the al___ ___abet song?

11. A crowd ga___ ___ered to watch the parade.

12. I like poa___ ___ed eggs.

13. Please re___ ___eck your work.

14. A go___ ___er dug tunnels under our lawn.

15. Your friend___ ___ip is important to me.

Notes for Home: Your child wrote consonant digraphs in the middle of words.
Home Activity: Take turns with your child writing other words with the letters *th, ch, ph,* or *sh* in the middle, leaving out the letters, and having the other person write the missing letters.

Name_____

A base word is a word without any prefixes, suffixes, or endings added.

	rerun	neighborhood	singing
Base Words:	run	neighbor	sing

Add the prefixes, suffixes, or endings shown to the base word to make new words.

lock

1. un + _____ = _____

2. _____ + ing = _____

3. _____ + er = _____

play

4. re + _____ = _____

5. _____ + ed = _____

6. _____ + er = _____

correct

7. in + _____ = _____

8. _____ + ing = _____

9. _____ + ion = _____

10. in + _____ + ly = _____

Notes for Home: Your child added prefixes, suffixes, and endings to base words.
Home Activity: Take turns with your child choosing a base word, adding a prefix, suffix, or ending, and then using the new word in a sentence.

When suffixes or endings are added to base words, the spelling of the base word sometimes changes.

Drop the final *e*.	come = coming
Double the final consonant.	run = running
Change *y* to *i*.	try = tries
No change	sing = singing

Write each word in the box that shows how the base word was changed.

armful	mysterious	lovable	biggest	worried
location	nearly	librarian	dirtiest	determination
approval	searches	hesitated	hidden	neighborhood
shutting	careful	memories	swimming	beginner

Drop the Final *e*	**Double the Final Consonant**
1. _____	6. _____
2. _____	7. _____
3. _____	8. _____
4. _____	9. _____
5. _____	10. _____
Change *y* to *i*	**No Change**
11. _____	16. _____
12. _____	17. _____
13. _____	18. _____
14. _____	19. _____
15. _____	20. _____

Notes for Home: Your child identified the spelling changes made to base words when suffixes or endings are added. **Home Activity:** Have your child add one more word to each list.

Consonants blends, such as *bl, gl,* and *st,* can stand for the beginning sound in a word.

Circle the blend that stands for the sound at the beginning of each picture name. Then write the blend to complete the word.

1. st
    sp

_____ _____ ar

2. gr
    gl

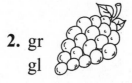

_____ _____ apes

3. pr
    pl

_____ _____ ane

4. fl
    fr

_____ _____ ower

5. dr
    tr

_____ _____ ill

6. fl
    fr

_____ _____ uit

7. sp
    st

_____ _____ ool

8. sm
    sn

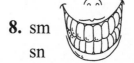

_____ _____ ile

9. bl
    br

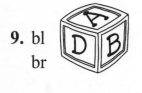

_____ _____ ock

10. gr
     gl

_____ _____ asses

Notes for Home: Your child identified initial consonant blends in words.
Home Activity: Choose a consonant blend from the page and name two words that begin with the blend. Then have your child choose a blend and name two words for it.

Consonant blends, such as *st, nt,* and *mp,* can stand for the ending sound in a word.

Circle the picture whose name has the ending sound spelled by the consonant blend.

1. nt     **2.** mp

3. st    **4.** st

5. nd    **6.** lt

7. mp    **8.** sk ...

9. nt    **10.** ld ...

 Notes for Home: Your child identified the final consonant blends in words.
Home Activity: Name a word that ends with a consonant blend. Write the letters that stand for the ending sound. Then ask your child to do the same.

Consonant blends can stand for the sound at the beginning of words.
Consonant blends can stand for the sound at the end of words.

Fill in the circle under the blend that begins or ends each picture name.

Beginning   **Ending**

1.    fr   br   tr   6.    mp   nd   nt
              ○   ○   ○   ○   ○   ○

2.    sn   st   sp   7.    lt   nd   ld
              ○   ○   ○   ○   ○   ○

3. 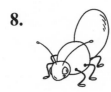   tr   gl   pr   8.   ct   lt   nt
              ○   ○   ○   ○   ○   ○

4.   sl   sm   st   9.   st   nt   lt
        ○   ○   ○   ○   ○   ○

5.    bl   pl   fl   10.    st   sk   nd
              ○   ○   ○   ○   ○   ○

Notes for Home: Your child identified initial or final consonant blends in picture names.
Home Activity: With your child, look through a newspaper. Circle words with beginning or ending blends.

Consonant digraphs, such as *th, ch, ph,* and *sh,* sometimes come in the middle of words. The two letters stand for one sound.

ano**th**er   rea**ch**ing   go**ph**er   fini**sh**ed

Write the word from the list that completes each sentence. Circle the digraph that is found in the middle of the word.

inchworm	father	telephone	feather	trophy
branches	washing	elephant	seashells	bookshelves
teacher	weather	bathtub	mushrooms	alphabet

1. Circus goes with _____.   th   ch   ph   sh

2. Prize goes with _____.   th   ch   ph   sh

3. Moth goes with _____.   th   ch   ph   sh

4. Mother goes with _____.   th   ch   ph   sh

5. School goes with _____.   th   ch   ph   sh

6. Beach goes with _____.   th   ch   ph   sh

7. Tree goes with _____.   th   ch   ph   sh

8. Library goes with _____.   th   ch   ph   sh

9. Rain goes with _____.   th   ch   ph   sh

10. ABC goes with _____.   th   ch   ph   sh

11. Cleaning goes with _____.   th   ch   ph   sh

12. Shower goes with _____.   th   ch   ph   sh

13. Call goes with _____.   th   ch   ph   sh

14. Bird goes with _____.   th   ch   ph   sh

15. Pizza goes with _____.   th   ch   ph   sh

Notes for Home: Your child identified consonant digraphs in the middle of words.
Home Activity: Go through the sentences together. Take turns giving another word that could complete each sentence.

Father, inchworm, elephant, and *fishing* all have consonant digraphs in the middle.

Circle the word in each question that has a *th, ch, ph,* or *sh* in the middle. Then use the circled word to write an answer to the question.

1. Where might you see an elephant?

   _____

2. What does a flashlight need to work?

   _____

3. Where do you put toothpaste?

   _____

4. What game do you play with your brother?

   _____

5. Where could you find a seashell?

   _____

6. What does a teacher do?

   _____

7. Who might win a trophy?

   _____

8. How do peaches taste?

   _____

9. What is the last letter of the alphabet?

   _____

10. What could you make in a workshop?

    _____

Notes for Home: Your child identified words with medial consonant digraphs.
Home Activity: Choose a circled word from the page and ask a question, using the word in the question. Have your child answer the question.

Some consonant blends, such as *scr, str,* and *spr,* have three letters. They can stand for the beginning sound in a word.

Circle the letters that stand for the beginning sound in the picture name. Add the circled letters to the letters shown to make a new word.

1.   str   spr

___ + eam = _____

2.   spl   spr

___ + ay = _____

3.   scr   spl

___ + een = _____

4.    squ   spl

___ + awk = _____

5.   str   spl

___ + ash = _____

6.   thr   spr

___ + one = _____

7.   scr   spl

___ + eech = _____

8.   spr   str

___ + eet = _____

9.   str   spr

___ + out = _____

10.   spr   thr

___ + oat = _____

Notes for Home: Your child identified three-letter consonant blends in words.
Home Activity: Look through a favorite storybook with your child. Find words with three-letter blends and tell what three letters begin each word.

Consonant blends with three letters, such as *spr, spl,* or *thr,* can come at the beginning of a word. The three letters stand for one sound.

Make new words. Change the underlined letter or letters in each word. Add the three-letter blend. Write the new word.

scr

1. <u>b</u>eam _____

2. <u>b</u>een _____

squ

3. <u>sp</u>eak _____

4. <u>s</u>neeze _____

spl

5. <u>w</u>inter _____

6. <u>c</u>rash _____

spr

7. <u>f</u>ling _____

8. <u>tw</u>inkle _____

str

9. <u>sw</u>eet _____

10. <u>ch</u>ange _____

thr

11. <u>m</u>ust _____

12. <u>c</u>oat _____

Complete each sentence. Use a word you wrote above.

13. When I am scared, I _____.

14. A mouse might make a _____.

15. The season before summer is _____.

16. I have a sore _____.

17. In a swimming pool, people like to _____.

18. Look both ways when crossing a _____.

19. A hug is a big _____.

20. A window might be covered by a _____.

Notes for Home: Your child wrote words with three-letter blends. **Home Activity:** Take turns with your child pointing to a three-letter blend and naming a word that begins with that blend.

Three-letter blends stand for the beginning sounds in these words.

squeak **str**eet **thr**ee

Write the word that answers the question. Circle the blend.

1. Does a mouse **scream** or **squeak?** _squeak_

2. Is **spring** or **string** a season? _spring_

3. Would you **sprig** or **splash** in a bathtub? _splash_

4. Are eggs usually **scrambled** or **scraped?** _scrambled_

5. Does a **screw** or a **scrap** hold something together? _screw_

6. Would a shirt have **stripes** or **scrunches?** _____

7. Does a backpack have a **strap** or a **sprain?** _____

8. Is a **square** or a **scream** a shape? _____

9. Do you **split** or **strain** wood? _____

10. Does a **splinter** or a **sprinkler** water a lawn? _____

11. Is **three** or **through** an age? _____

12. Might a cat **squeeze** or **scratch** you? _____

13. Could a **throat** or a **throne** feel sore? _____

14. Might you **sprout** or **sprain** an ankle? _____

15. Would you **scrub** or **scratch** a floor to make it clean? _____

Notes for Home: Your child identified words with three-letter blends.
Home Activity: Have your child use each word he or she wrote in a sentence.

A consonant blend can stand for the sound at the beginning or end of a word.

drum   **cl**oud   **sm**all

ha**nd**   a**sk**   co**ld**

Write each word in the box where it belongs. Then write the blend or blends found in the words.

mask	meant	gleam	gold	friend
train	lamp	bend	plate	vest
guest	dry	smile	risk	spider
greed	crust	scout	belt	steam

Beginning Blends

1. _____ _____

2. _____ _____

3. _____ _____

4. _____ _____

5. _____ _____

6. _____ _____

7. _____ _____

8. _____ _____

9. _____ _____

Ending Blends

10. _____ _____

11. _____ _____

12. _____ _____

13. _____ _____

14. _____ _____

15. _____ _____

16. _____ _____

17. _____ _____

18. _____ _____

Both Beginning and Ending Blends

19. _____ _____ _____

20. _____ _____ _____

Notes for Home: Your child wrote words with initial and final consonant blends.
Home Activity: Ask your child to choose a word from the page and to name another word with the same beginning or ending blend. Then you take a turn.

A consonant blend can stand for the sound at the beginning or end of a word.

drum   **gr**apes   **pl**ate   ha**nd**   ma**sk**   sta**mp**

Circle the blend in each word. Then write the words where they belong in the sentence. Some words will not be used.

snow   melt   sand

1. The _____ began to _____ in the sun.

toast   grapes   skates

2. We ate juicy _____ and crunchy _____.

belt   nest   dress

3. Mom bought a _____ and a _____.

lamp   plane   cloud

4. I saw a _____ and a _____ in the sky.

sweep   broom   spoon

5. Get a _____ and _____ the floor.

© Scott Foresman 3

Notes for Home: Your child wrote words with initial and final consonant blends.
Home Activity: Have your child choose three words from the page and use any two of the words to make a new sentence.

Name _____

The letters *oi* and *oy* stand for the vowel sound in these words.

co**in**   **b**o**y**

Write the word that completes each phrase. Circle the letters that stand for the vowel sound.

joy	noise	choice	enjoy	join
point	royal	cowboy	toy	voyage
soil	loyal	oil	voice	annoying

1. a _____ to play with   oi   oy

2. full of happiness and _____   oi   oy

3. need _____ for the squeak   oi   oy

4. to _____ the two ends   oi   oy

5. seeds growing in _____   oi   oy

6. a loud _____   oi   oy

7. the _____ prince and princess   oi   oy

8. her beautiful singing _____   oi   oy

9. a broken pencil _____   oi   oy

10. that _____ rounding up cattle   oi   oy

11. an _____ buzzing sound   oi   oy

12. a _____ between two things   oi   oy

13. a _____ across the ocean   oi   oy

14. to _____ the movie   oi   oy

15. a _____ fan of the football team   oi   oy

Notes for Home: Your child wrote words with the vowel diphthongs *oi* and *oy*.
Home Activity: Take turns with your child using the phrases on the page to make sentences.
Then pick one sentence and use it to begin a story that you make up together.

© Scott Foresman 3

The letters *oi* and *oy* stand for the vowel sound in *soil* and *boy*.

Write the word from the list that rhymes with the word in the box. Circle the letters that stand for the vowel sound. Then follow the directions.

enjoy   disappoint   royal   coin   voice

1. | join | _____   oi   oy

Add *-ed* to the end of each word.

_____   _____

2. | loyal | _____   oi   oy

Add *-ty* to the end of each word.

_____   _____

3. | employ | _____   oi   oy

Add *-ment* to the end of each word.

_____   _____

4. | anoint | _____   oi   oy

Add *-ing* to the end of each word.

_____   _____

5. | rejoice | _____   oi   oy

Take off the final *e* and add *-ing* to each word.

_____   _____

Notes for Home: Your child wrote words with the vowel diphthongs *oi* and *oy*.
Home Activity: Together list other words that have *oi* or *oy* in them. Take turns with your child naming words that rhyme with the words in the list.

Oil and *joy* have the same vowel sound. The letters *oi* and *oy* stand for that vowel sound.

Write a word from the list next to the word that is almost alike in meaning. Circle the letters that stand for the vowel sound you hear in *oil*.

loyal	toy	toil	oyster
joyful	spoil	join	voyage

1. happy _____

2. rot _____

3. faithful _____

4. plaything _____

5. connect _____

6. work _____

7. shellfish _____

8. trip _____

Write a word from the list next to the word that is opposite in meaning. Circle the letters that stand for the vowel sound you hear in *oil*.

destroy	moist	loyal	noisy
boy	unemployed	joy	

9. sadness _____

10. girl _____

11. dry _____

12. build _____

13. quiet _____

14. employed _____

15. disloyal _____

Notes for Home: Your child wrote words with the vowel diphthongs *oi* and *oy*.
Home Activity: Have your child look through newspaper and magazine ads for words with *oi* and *oy*. Read the words together.

© Scott Foresman 3

Name_____

A consonant blend with three letters, such as *str, spl,* or *thr,* stands for one sound.

string **spl**ash **thr**ee

Use the clues to complete the puzzle.

| thread | sprinkler | square | strikes | strawberry |
| scream | scrub | three | streets | splash |

Across

1. used to water a lawn

2. in baseball, three and you are out

5. to wash something by rubbing it hard

6. a red fruit

8. a shape with four equal sides

Down

1. places where cars drive

3. use a needle to sew with this

4. a loud, high yell

5. something people do in a swimming pool

7. the number between two and four

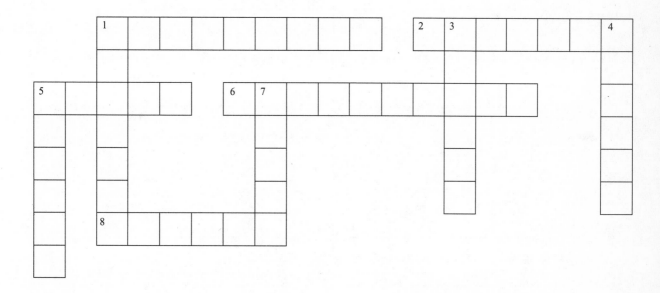

Notes for Home: Your child completed a puzzle, using words with three-letter blends.
Home Activity: Have your child choose one of these blends: *scr, spl, str, squ, spr, thr.*
Together write as many words as you can that begin with the blend.

A consonant blend may have three letters that stand for one sound.

scream **squ**are **thr**ee

Write each word in the box that has the same three-letter blend.

strong	spring	splash	string	squeak
thrill	throw	stream	squirrel	spray
splinter	square	spread	thread	straw
scratch	split	scream	scrub	three

scr	**spl**
1. _____	4. _____
2. _____	5. _____
3. _____	6. _____
spr	**squ**
7. _____	10. _____
8. _____	11. _____
9. _____	12. _____
str	**thr**
13. _____	17. _____
14. _____	18. _____
15. _____	19. _____
16. _____	20. _____

Notes for Home: Your child sorted words with three-letter blends. **Home Activity:** Take turns with your child choosing any three words from the list at the top of the page and putting the words in alphabetical order.

A possessive shows that something belongs to someone or something.

    • Add *'s* to make a singular noun possessive.   doctor   doctor**'s**
    • Add *'s* to make a plural noun possessive.   men   men**'s**
    • Add *'* to a plural noun that ends in *s*.   twins   twins**'**

Make each singular or plural noun possessive.

1. girl _____

2. boy _____

3. Maria _____

4. Lee _____

5. children _____

6. family _____

7. book _____

8. tiger _____

9. herd _____

10. flock _____

Make each plural noun possessive.

11. dogs _____

12. teachers _____

13. shells _____

14. girls _____

15. mice _____

16. geese _____

17. bunnies _____

18. women _____

19. foxes _____

20. cities _____

Notes for Home: Your child wrote possessive forms of singular and plural nouns.
Home Activity: Point to an object. Ask your child to name the object, write its name, say the possessive, and then write it. Example: *book, book's.*

A possessive shows that something belongs to someone or something.

   • Add *'s* to make a singular noun possessive.   cat   cat's
   • Add *'s* to make a plural noun possessive.   mice   mice's
   • Add *'* to a plural noun that ends in *s*.   dogs   dogs'

Change each phrase into a phrase with a possessive.

   Example: the stripes of the tiger = the tiger's stripes

1. the tractor that belongs to the farmer   _____

2. a pool for the penguins   _____

3. a pencil that Keesha owns   _____

4. that game that the twins own   _____

5. some seed for the parrots   _____

6. the book belonging to Juan   _____

7. this car belonging to that family   _____

8. a ball that the cat has   _____

9. the flowers belonging to those people   _____

10. the chains for the necklaces   _____

11. a bike for Kwan   _____

12. the park belonging to the community   _____

13. some cages for the lions   _____

14. some shoes belonging to the children   _____

15. this report belonging to the group   _____

Notes for Home: Your child wrote phrases with possessives. **Home Activity:** Take turns with your child writing possessive phrases, such as *Mary's book* or *the dogs' bones*.

Here is how to make nouns possessive:

singular noun	sister	sister**'s**
plural noun	women	women**'s**
plural noun ending in *s*	brothers	brothers**'**

Write the possessive noun in each phrase. After each noun, write **S** for singular noun or **P** for plural noun.

1. doctor's office   **2.** children's games

_____ _____   _____ _____

3. sisters' friend   **4.** lion's paw

_____ _____   _____ _____

5. men's hats   **6.** woman's picture

_____ _____   _____ _____

Rewrite each sentence. Use the possessive form of the noun in parentheses.

7. We had a party for my ___ anniversary. (parents)

_____

8. My ___ family came from Tampa. (mother)

_____

9. ___ brother flew in from Dallas. (Dad)

_____

10. Our ___ celebration was a big success. (family)

_____

© Scott Foresman 3

Notes for Home: Your child identified and wrote possessive nouns.
Home Activity: Have your child look through a favorite book for examples of possessives and tell who owns what.

The letters *oi* and *oy* stand for the vowel sound in *join* and *toy*.

Read each sentence. Write one or two words that have the same vowel sound as *join* and *toy*.

The boys made a lot of noise playing in the yard.

1. _____   2. _____

First, boil the potatoes, and then wrap them in foil.

3. _____   4. _____

Try to join these two coils of rope.

5. _____   6. _____

The cowboy had a loud singing voice.

7. _____   8. _____

The loyal worker was a good employee.

9. _____   10. _____

An oyster tastes good dipped in soy sauce.

11. _____   12. _____

The family enjoyed the sea voyage.

13. _____   14. _____

Use oil to fix the door hinge.

15. _____

Notes for Home: Your child identified and wrote words with *oi* and *oy*.
Home Activity: Have your child choose two words he or she wrote on the page and make up a new sentence using the words.

The letters *oi* and *oy* stand for the vowel sound in *join* and *toy*.

Circle 12 hidden words with *oi* and *oy*. Write the words you circle.
Hint: Two words are small words within bigger words.

t	o	y	b	c	m	o	i	s	t	p	o	i	n	t
d	e	f	g	s	p	o	i	l	n	o	i	s	e	h
k	l	b	o	y	m	p	r	s	j	o	y	f	u	l
l	o	y	a	l	s	v	o	i	c	e	g	d	n	s
r	h	v	o	y	a	g	e	b	f	h	m	k	r	s

1. _____   2. _____

3. _____   4. _____

5. _____   6. _____

7. _____   8. _____

9. _____   10. _____

11. _____   12. _____

Write the word from above that means the same as the phrase.

13. a plaything   _____

14. the tip of a pencil   _____

15. very happy   _____

Notes for Home: Your child wrote words with *oi* and *oy*. **Home Activity:** Together make a word-search puzzle like the one on the page. Use words with *oi* and *oy*.

Name_____

The letters *ar, er, ir, or,* and *ur* stand for the vowel sounds in these words.

| card | her | third | born | turn |

Write the word that answers each question. Then write the letters that stand for the vowel-*r* sound in the word.

1. Do you eat with a fort or a fork? _____ _____

2. Would you sir or stir pancake batter? _____ _____

3. Might you sit on a front port or porch? _____ _____

4. Does a rabbit have fur or spurs? _____ _____

5. Could you see a star or a start in the sky? _____ _____

6. Do you drink water because you are thirsty or thirty? _____ _____

7. Is a gift for or forth someone? _____ _____

8. Would you turn or burn a candle for light? _____ _____

9. Do ferns or terms grow in the woods? _____ _____

10. Does a shirt or a skirt have sleeves? _____ _____

Notes for Home: Your child wrote vowel-*r* words and identified vowel-*r* spellings.
Home Activity: With your child, look through newspapers. Have your child use a crayon to circle words with *ar, er, ir, or,* and *ur.*

The letters *ar, er, ir, or,* and *ur* stand for the vowel sounds in these words.

| st**ar**t | h**er** | f**ir**st | f**or** | t**ur**n |

Write the word from the box that rhymes with each picture name. Then write the letters that stand for the vowel-*r* sound.

| cork | stern | third | fur | dirt |
| jar | thorn | nurse | farm | bark |

1.   _____ ____

2.   _____ ____

3.   _____ ____

4.   _____ ____

5.   _____ ____

6.   _____ ____

7.   _____ ____

8. 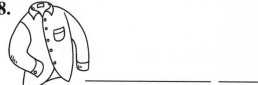 _____ ____

9. _____ ____

10.  _____ ____

 Notes for Home: Your child wrote *r*-controlled vowel words. **Home Activity:** Take turns with your child drawing pictures of things whose names have *r*-controlled vowel sounds. Help each other write the name for each picture.

The letters *ear* and *our* stand for the vowel sounds in these words

learn   **four**

Write each word under the word that has the same vowel-*r* sound. Some words will not be written.

early	pour	court	our	fear
clear	source	heard	course	earth
earn	hour	mourn	search	hear

learn   **four**

1. _____   6. _____

2. _____   7. _____

3. _____   8. _____

4. _____   9. _____

5. _____   10. _____

Write the word from above that completes each phrase.

11. morning and evening; late and _____

12. football and field; basketball and _____

13. locate and seek; find and _____

14. laugh and rejoice; cry and _____

15. looked and saw; listened and _____

Notes for Home: Your child sorted and wrote words with the *r*-controlled vowel patterns *ear* and *our*. **Home Activity:** Use the words in the lists to make up a silly story together.

Suffixes are added to the ends of words.

| kind**ness** | bright**ly** | help**ful** | humor**ous** |

Use a word from the box to complete each tongue twister. Then write the suffix that appears at the end of the word.

> sadly   finally   powerful   delightful   poisonous
> glamorous   greatness   lively   illness   wonderful

1. Leo Lion likes _____ leaps.   _____

2. Wendy's _____ wagon won.   _____

3. Greta's _____ grew gradually.   _____

4. Firefighters _____ found frisky Fluffy.   _____

5. Sarah sat _____ on the soft, silky sofa.   _____

6. Dora dug _____, dainty daffodils.   _____

7. Inez's _____ is itchy and infectious.   _____

8. Please pull perilous, pesky, _____ plants.   _____

9. Gloria's glimmering, _____ gloves glittered.   _____

10. Pretty, _____ ponies pulled the plows.   _____

Notes for Home: Your child wrote words with suffixes. **Home Activity:** Take turns with your child saying tongue twisters you know. Then make up some tongue twisters that have words with suffixes.

Sometimes when a suffix is added to the end of a word, a spelling change is needed. Sometimes no spelling change is needed.

No spelling change is needed.   kind + ness = kindness

If a word ends in *y*, the *y* is changed to *i*.   beauty − y + i + ful = beautiful

Underline the answer to the question. Write the new word.

1.   **bright**

Does the word end in *y*?   Yes   No

Add **ly.** Write the word.

_____

2.   **happy**

Does the word end in *y*?   Yes   No

Add **ness.** Write the word.

_____

3.   **angry**

Does the word end in *y*?   Yes   No

Add **ly.** Write the word.

_____

4.   **marvel**

Does the word end in *y*?   Yes   No

Add **ous.** Write the word.

_____

5.   **humor**

Does the word end in *y*?   Yes   No

Add **ous.** Write the word.

_____

6.   **fury**

Does the word end in *y*?   Yes   No

Add **ous.** Write the word.

_____

7.   **danger**

Does the word end in *y*?   Yes   No

Add **ous.** Write the word.

_____

8.   **empty**

Does the word end in *y*?   Yes   No

Add **ness.** Write the word.

_____

9.   **easy**

Does the word end in *y*?   Yes   No

Add **ly.** Write the word.

_____

10.   **power**

Does the word end in *y*?   Yes   No

Add **ful.** Write the word.

_____

Notes for Home: Your child added suffixes to words, making spelling changes if necessary. **Home Activity:** Have your child make up a sentence for each word he or she wrote on the page.

Nouns that name more than one person, place, or thing are called plural nouns.

- Add -*s* to most nouns to make them plural.   dog   dog**s**
- Add -*es* to nouns that end in *s, ss, x, ch,* and *sh.*   lunch   lunch**es**

Write the plural of each noun.

1. plane _____

2. pilot _____

3. field _____

4. box _____

5. wish _____

6. paper _____

7. glass _____

8. shed _____

9. brush _____

10. beach _____

11. week _____

12. push _____

13. pass _____

14. friend _____

15. circus _____

Use words you wrote above to complete the sentences.

16. The _____ landed the plane safely.

17. Corn is growing in those _____.

18. How many _____ are in a year?

19. He drank two _____ of milk.

20. How many _____ of cereal are on the shelf?

© Scott Foresman 3

Notes for Home: Your child formed the plurals of words by adding *s* or *es*.
Home Activity: Take turns with your child pointing to an object, saying the plural form of its name, and writing the plural form.

Name_____

If a word ends in a vowel and *y, -s* is added to make the word mean more than one.

monk**ey** + s = monkey**s**

If a word ends in a consonant and *y,* the *y* is changed to *i,* and *-es* is added to make the word mean more than one.

ba**by** – y + i + es = ba**bies**

Underline *vowel* or *consonant* to answer the question. Then add *-s* or *-es* and write the plural form of the word.

Word	Question	Plural
1. day	Is the letter before *y* a vowel or a consonant?	_____
2. toy	Is the letter before *y* a vowel or a consonant?	_____
3. puppy	Is the letter before *y* a vowel or a consonant?	_____
4. key	Is the letter before *y* a vowel or a consonant?	_____
5. berry	Is the letter before *y* a vowel or a consonant?	_____
6. boy	Is the letter before *y* a vowel or a consonant?	_____
7. bunny	Is the letter before *y* a vowel or a consonant?	_____
8. city	Is the letter before *y* a vowel or a consonant?	_____
9. body	Is the letter before *y* a vowel or a consonant?	_____
10. delay	Is the letter before *y* a vowel or a consonant?	_____

Notes for Home: Your child wrote the plural forms of words ending in *y*.
Home Activity: With your child, look for nouns that end in *y*. Tell how to make the plural. Use the question on the page to help decide whether to make a spelling change.

Name_____

Some nouns make their plurals in unusual ways.

    1. If the noun ends in *f* or *fe,* the *f* or *fe*
       is changed to *v*, and *-es* is added.   shel**f**   shel**ves**
    2. Some nouns use a new word.   man   men
    3. Some nouns use the same word.   deer   deer

Write **1, 2,** or **3** to tell how each plural was formed. Use the numbered list above.

  1. mouse/mice _____   **2.** sheep/sheep _____

  3. wolf/wolves _____   **4.** woman/women _____

  5. child/children _____   **6.** foot/feet _____

  7. knife/knives _____   **8.** leaf/leaves _____

  9. calf/calves _____   **10.** goose/geese _____

Write **1, 2,** or **3** to show how to make each word plural. Then write the new word.

  11. wife _____ _____

  12. tooth _____ _____

  13. moose _____ _____

  14. loaf _____ _____

  15. gentleman _____ _____

Notes for Home: Your child wrote the plural forms of nouns whose plurals are formed in unusual ways. **Home Activity:** Have your child look in newspapers for plural nouns and tell how each plural was formed. Use the numbered list on the page for help.

Name_____

Remember how possessive nouns are made:

- For a singular noun, add *'s*.   aunt   aunt**'s**
- For a plural noun, add *'s*.   men   men**'s**
- For a plural noun that ends in *s,* add *'*.   uncles   uncles**'**

Write the possessive of the word in parentheses to complete each phrase.

1. (pony)   the _____ mane

2. (schools)   the _____ flags

3. (Smith)   Mrs. _____ house

4. (children)   the _____ books

5. (girls)   the _____ shoes

6. (workers)   the _____ tools

7. (men)   the _____ races

8. (fox)   the _____ tail

9. (sheep)   the _____ wool

10. (women)   the _____ hats

Notes for Home: Your child wrote singular and plural possessive nouns.
Home Activity: Have your child name a person and something he or she might own and then write the name and the object in a possessive phrase. Example: *Mary book, Mary's book.*

Name_____

A possessive shows that something belongs to someone or something.

- Add *'s* to make a singular noun possessive.   neighbor   neighbor**'s**
- Add *'s* to make a plural noun possessive.   people   people**'s**
- Add *'* to a plural noun that ends in *s*.   planes   planes**'**

Write the possessive form of each noun. Then add a word to show something that is owned.

Example: swan   swan's   swan's feathers

1. boy   _____   _____

2. cats   _____   _____

3. men   _____   _____

4. mothers   _____   _____

5. bird   _____   _____

6. children   _____   _____

7. turtles   _____   _____

8. teachers   _____   _____

9. chair   _____   _____

10. sister   _____   _____

11. women   _____   _____

12. tree   _____   _____

13. sheep   _____   _____

14. insects   _____   _____

15. mice   _____   _____

© Scott Foresman 3

Notes for Home: Your child wrote possessive nouns and possessive phrases.
Home Activity: Take turns with your child using the possessive phrases he or she wrote to create oral sentences. Tell which word is the possessive and whether it is singular or plural.

Name _____

The *k* sound can be spelled by the letters *c, ck,* or *ch.*

color   ne**ck**   **ch**ord

Sort the words to show what letter or letters stand for /k/ in each word.

back	ache	can	stomach	careful
thick	because	cut	vacation	coat
anchor	traffic	echo	track	wreck
bucket	fact	clock	count	recall

/k/ = c

1. _____   2. _____

3. _____   4. _____

5. _____   6. _____

7. _____   8. _____

9. _____   10. _____

/k/ = ck

11. _____   12. _____

13. _____   14. _____

15. _____   16. _____

/k/ = ch

17. _____   18. _____

19. _____   20. _____

Notes for Home: Your child wrote words with /k/ spelled *c, ck,* or *ch.*
Home Activity: With your child, look through the Yellow Pages in a telephone book for words with /k/ spelled *c, ck,* or *ch.*

The letters *c*, *ck*, and *ch* stand for the *k* sound in these words.

                cat   **duck**   **ache**

Write the word in the sentence with /k/. Circle the letter or letters that stand for /k/.

1. Where is my other green sock?   _____

2. My stomach feels full.   _____

3. The chorus sang a happy song.   _____

4. This bucket of water is heavy.   _____

5. My tooth ached all night.   _____

6. Have you ever been camping?   _____

7. Someone left a red jacket on the bus.   _____

8. How high did he count?   _____

9. My friend drives a big truck.   _____

10. What is the name of that chord?   _____

11. The traffic was heavy today.   _____

12. I heard the echo of my voice.   _____

13. My uncle lives in Ohio.   _____

14. What caused the lamp to fall?   _____

15. We need an anchor for the boat.   _____

Notes for Home: Your child identified and wrote words with /k/ spelled *c*, *ck*, or *ch*.
Home Activity: Have your child choose two /k/ words he or she wrote on the page and use the words in a sentence.

Name _____

The letters *ar, er, ir, or,* and *ur* stand for the vowel sounds in these words.

car   **her**   **bir**d   **horn**   **turn**

Write the word that belongs in each statement. Then write the letters that stand for the vowel-*r* sound.

nurse   star   circus   verses   storm
barn   ferns   horse   birthday   fur

1. Farmer: "Every morning I let the cows out of
   the _____." _____

2. Doctor: "The _____ will give you your shot." _____

3. Astronomer: "Light from that _____ takes
   millions of light-years to reach Earth." _____

4. Vet: "You need to brush your cat's _____." _____

5. Gardener: "I find that _____ grow best
   in shady, moist places." _____

6. Baker: "Do you want vanilla or chocolate icing on this
   _____ cake?" _____

7. Ringmaster: "Welcome to the _____." _____

8. Jockey: "I knew my _____ could win the race." _____

9. Poet: "My new poem has seven _____." _____

10. Weather Forecaster: "We are expecting a major
    _____ with heavy rain and high winds." _____

Notes for Home: Your child wrote words with *r*-controlled vowels. **Home Activity:** Help
your child make up a new sentence for each word written on the page.

108

The letters *air* and *are* stand for the vowel sound in these words.

ch**air**   d**are**

Write the words in the correct order to make sentences. Circle the words with the vowel patterns *air* and *are*.

1. careful Be walking the across street.

_____

2. scared That growling dog me.

_____

3. friends to fair Our the drove us.

_____

4. takes her good She care of goldfish.

_____

5. ice slick the made The stairs.

_____

6. very has ears A long hare.

_____

7. baby silky The blond has hair.

_____

8. a pair got new shoes I of.

_____

9. have a tire spare in Always the car.

_____

10. a flair has for Rosa painting.

_____

Notes for Home: Your child wrote sentences with *air* and *are* words.
Home Activity: Take turns with your child writing a scrambled sentence with an *air* or *are* word and having the other person unscramble the sentence.

The letters *ear* and *our* stand for the vowel sounds in these words.

n*ear* **l*ear*n** **g*our*d**

Write the word that goes with the clue. Write the letters that stand for the vowel-*r* sound.

early	hear	mourn	course	fourth
four	source	search	year	court
fear	earth	earn	pour	dear

1. do this with your ears   _____ _____

2. the number after three   _____ _____

3. where something comes from   _____ _____

4. 52 weeks in this   _____ _____

5. the opposite of *late*   _____ _____

6. a path followed   _____ _____

7. to look for   _____ _____

8. a word for *soil*   _____ _____

9. do this with milk   _____ _____

10. a scared feeling   _____ _____

11. feel sad about something   _____ _____

12. to make money   _____ _____

13. a place with judges   _____ _____

14. the place after third   _____ _____

15. word to begin a letter   _____ _____

Notes for Home: Your child wrote words with the vowel patterns *ear* and *our*.
Home Activity: Help your child make a list of words with the vowel sounds and patterns in *near*, *learn*, and *four*. Have your child read the words and name words that rhyme.

Name_____

When a prefix is added to the beginning of a word, it changes the meaning of the word.

possible	able to be done	**im**possible	**not** able to be done
honest	truthful	**dis**honest	**not** truthful
living	alive	**non**living	**not** alive

Write the word from the box that has the prefix and meaning shown.

| imperfect | disloyal | immovable | nonstop | nonbreakable |
| disappear | nonresident | disapprove | impolite | impatient |

1. dis + faithful

_____

2. im + able to change its place

_____

3. non + able to be broken

_____

4. im + showing manners

_____

5. dis + come into sight

_____

6. dis + be in favor of

_____

7. non + a person living in a place

_____

8. non + will not halt

_____

9. im + having no mistakes

_____

10. im + willing to wait

_____

Notes for Home: Your child wrote words with the prefixes *im-*, *dis-*, and *non-*.
Home Activity: Have your child name some other words with the prefixes *im-*, *dis-*, and *non-* and tell what the words mean. Use a dictionary for help.

When a prefix is added to the beginning of a word, the spelling of the word does not change.

im + polite = impolite
dis + appear = disappear
non + living = nonliving

Add _im-_, _dis-_, or _non-_ to each word to make a new word. Write the new word.

1. possible _____

2. please _____

3. agree _____

4. stop _____

5. fiction _____

6. practical _____

7. honest _____

8. fat _____

9. patient _____

10. proper _____

Sort the words you wrote above according to their prefixes.

dis-

non-

11. _____

14. _____

12. _____

15. _____

13. _____

16. _____

im-

17. _____

18. _____

19. _____

20. _____

Notes for Home: Your child added the prefixes _im-_, _dis-_, and _non-_ to words.
Home Activity: Take turns with your child using the words he or she wrote on the page in oral sentences.

Name_____

Prefixes, such as *im-*, *dis-*, and *non-*, change the meanings of words.

im + polite	**im**polite	not polite
dis + honest	**dis**honest	not honest
non + breakable	**non**breakable	not breakable

Write the opposite of each word by circling the correct prefix and writing the new word.

Prefixes			**Word**	**Word with Prefix**
1. im	dis	non	please	_____
2. im	dis	non	possible	_____
3. im	dis	non	stop	_____
4. im	dis	non	like	_____
5. im	dis	non	patient	_____
6. im	dis	non	living	_____
7. im	dis	non	loyal	_____
8. im	dis	non	practical	_____
9. im	dis	non	sense	_____
10. im	dis	non	approve	_____

Notes for Home: Your child added the prefixes *im-*, *dis-*, and *non-* to words.
Home Activity: Help your child name words that are opposites. Use some words that begin with *im-*, *dis-*, and *non-*.

Plural nouns can be made in several ways.

- The plurals of most nouns are formed by adding -*s* or -*es*.
- If a noun ends in a vowel and *y, s* is added.
- If a noun ends in a consonant and *y,* the *y* is changed to *i,* and -*es* is added.
- The plurals of words ending in *s, ss, x, ch,* or *sh* are formed by adding -*es*.

Write the plural form of the word in parentheses.

1. Our (family) like to have picnics.   _____

2. We all help make the picnic (lunch).   _____

3. My sister likes fruit (salad).   _____

4. I like chicken (sandwich).   _____

5. Dad says we must always bring (cherry).   _____

6. Mom loves cool (glass) of lemonade.   _____

7. We usually have the picnics on (holiday).   _____

8. Each family brings (box) of balls and bats.   _____

9. The boys play on (team) against the girls.   _____

10. These (day) together are wonderful.   _____

Notes for Home: Your child formed the plurals of nouns. **Home Activity:** Together talk about food you both like to eat at picnics. Use plurals as you talk.

© Scott Foresman 3

Name_____

Some nouns have special plurals.

- The plurals of nouns that end in *f* and *fe* are
  formed by changing *f* or *fe* to *v* and adding *-es*.   shel**f**   shel**ves**
- Sometimes a new word is used for the plural.   man   men
- Sometimes the singular and plural forms are the same.   scissors   scissors

Sort the words to show how each plural was formed.

teeth	women	calves	mice	knives
leaves	sheep	children	wolves	moose
deer	geese	loaves	selves	feet

The *f* or *fe* was changed to *v*. Then *-es* was added.

1. _____   2. _____

3. _____   4. _____

5. _____   6. _____

A new word was used.

7. _____   8. _____

9. _____   10. _____

11. _____   12. _____

The same word is used for singular and plural.

13. _____   14. _____

15. _____

Notes for Home: Your child sorted words to show how plurals were formed.
Home Activity: Work together with your child to add more words to the lists.

When adding the ending *-ed* or *-ing* to words, sometimes a spelling change is needed.

no change	jump	jump**ed**	jump**ing**
drop the final *e*	hope	hop**ed**	hop**ing**
double the final consonant	stop	stop**ped**	stop**ping**
change final *y* to *i*	cry	**cried**	
no change	cry	cr**ying**	

Add the ending shown. Write the new word.

Make No Spelling Change

1. watch (ed) _____

2. lift (ing) _____

3. pack (ed) _____

4. try (ing) _____

5. deny (ing) _____

Drop the Final *e*

6. like (ed) _____

7. save (ed) _____

8. smile (ing) _____

9. tire (ed) _____

10. shine (ing) _____

Double the Final Consonant

11. plan (ed) _____

12. drip (ed) _____

13. run (ing) _____

14. swim (ing) _____

15. get (ing) _____

Change *y* to *i*

16. dry (ed) _____

17. worry (ed) _____

18. supply (ed) _____

19. try (ed) _____

20. hurry (ing) _____

Notes for Home: Your child added *-ed* and *-ing* to words. **Home Activity:** Together look through a newspaper or book to find words ending in *-ed* or *-ing*. Have your child tell whether a spelling change was needed when the ending was added to each word.

Name_____

When the endings *-er* and *-est* are added to words, a spelling change may be needed.

1. no change	great	great**er**	great**est**
2. drop the final *e*	larg**e**	larg**er**	larg**est**
3. double the final consonant	bi**g**	big**ger**	big**gest**
4. change final *y* to *i*	happy	happ**ier**	happ**iest**

Write the opposite of each word. Use words from the list. Write **1, 2, 3,** or **4** to show what spelling change, if any, was needed when the ending was added to the answer word.

bigger	easier	hottest	saddest	largest
lightest	driest	youngest	shortest	widest

1. tallest

_____ _____

2. happiest

_____ _____

3. smaller

_____ _____

4. darkest

_____ _____

5. coldest

_____ _____

6. smallest

_____ _____

7. harder

_____ _____

8. oldest

_____ _____

9. narrowest

_____ _____

10. wettest

_____ _____

Notes for Home: Your child wrote words with *-er* and *-est*. **Home Activity:** Name a word ending in *-er* or *-est,* and have your child give its opposite. Then have your child name an *-er* or *-est* word and you give its opposite.

Name_____

The ending *-er* can be added to words to make them mean "more." The ending *-est* can be added to words to make them mean "most."

deep   deep**er** (more deep)   deep**est** (most deep)

Write the *-er* and *-est* forms of each word. Remember to make these spelling changes if they are needed.

drop the final *e*	large	larg**er**	larg**est**
double the final consonant	big	big**ger**	big**gest**
change final *y* to *i*	happy	happ**ier**	happ**iest**

Word	**More**	**Most**
1. slow	_____	_____
2. funny	_____	_____
3. sad	_____	_____
4. lazy	_____	_____
5. flat	_____	_____
6. brave	_____	_____
7. clean	_____	_____
8. hot	_____	_____
9. easy	_____	_____
10. tame	_____	_____

Notes for Home: Your child wrote words with *-er* and *-est*. **Home Activity:** Work together with your child. Choose a word from the page. Use all three forms in a sentence like this: *I was slow, she was slower, but he was slowest of all.*

The letters *c, ck,* and *ch* spell the *k* sound in these words.

can   **du*ck***   **a*ch*e**

Underline the word in each group that has /k/. In the box, write the letter or letters that stand for /k/ in the word you underlined.

1. cover

city

ice

2. chair

echo

inch

3. lock

cheer

pencil

4. cent

face

uncle

5. chord

chain

teach

6. peace

stick

cheese

7. fact

center

dance

8. chase

anchor

reach

9. each

lettuce

pocket

10. decide

fancy

music

Notes for Home: Your child identified words with /k/ spelled *c, ck,* and *ch*.
Home Activity: Take turns with your child giving a meaning clue or a synonym for each underlined word and having the other person name the word.

The letters *c, ck,* and *ch* spell /k/ in *color, dock,* and *ache.*

Write the word that goes with the two words shown. Write the letter or letters that stand for /k/.

cousin	corn	rock	cover	stomach
jacket	complete	truck	cool	bucket
colt	chorus	anchor	duck	trick

1. car, bus

_____ _____

2. mast, deck

_____ _____

3. beans, peas

_____ _____

4. pail, can

_____ _____

5. heart, lungs

_____ _____

6. coat, sweater

_____ _____

7. joke, prank

_____ _____

8. lid, top

_____ _____

9. aunt, uncle

_____ _____

10. calf, lamb

_____ _____

11. cold, chilly

_____ _____

12. singers, choir

_____ _____

13. stone, pebble

_____ _____

14. finish, end

_____ _____

15. goose, swan

_____ _____

Notes for Home: Your child wrote words in which /k/ is spelled *c, ck,* or *ch.*
Home Activity: Take turns with your child naming three things that go together in some way.

Name _____

The letters *wh* stand for the sounds at the beginning of these words.

what   **wh**o

Read each word. Circle *what* if the *wh* in the word sounds like the *wh* in *what*.
Circle *who* if the *wh* in the word sounds like the *wh* in *who*.

1.   **white**   2.   **why**   3.   **whole**

   what   who   what   who   what   who

4.   **wheat**   5.   **whom**   6.   **wheel**

   what   who   what   who   what   who

7.   **whose**   8.   **when**   9.   **where**

   what   who   what   who   what   who

10.   **which**   11.   **whoever**   12.   **while**

   what   who   what   who   what   who

13.   **whirl**   14.   **wholesome**   15.   **whistle**

   what   who   what   who   what   who

 Notes for Home: Your child identified words in which *wh* stands for two different sounds.
Home Activity: Together use the words *who, what, when, where,* and *why* to ask each other
questions.

The letters *wh* stand for the beginning sound in *wheel*.
The letters *wh* stand for the beginning sound in *whole*.

Write the words in which *wh* stands for the sound in *wheel* around the wheel. Write the words in which *wh* stands for the sound in *whole* on the loaf of whole-wheat bread.

white	who	when	why	whoever
what	where	whirl	whose	whom

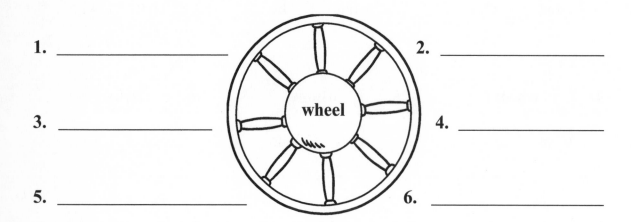

1. _____

2. _____

3. _____

wheel

4. _____

5. _____

6. _____

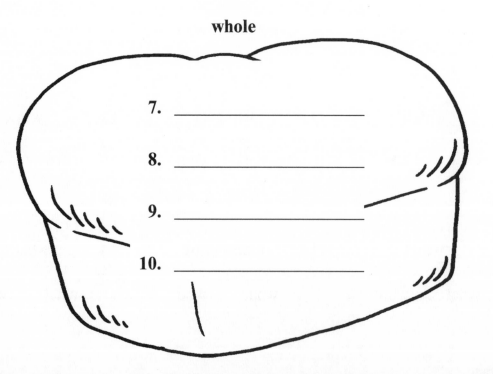

whole

7. _____

8. _____

9. _____

10. _____

Notes for Home: Your child wrote words in which *wh* stands for the sounds in *wheel* and *whole*. **Home Activity:** Take turns with your child scrambling one of the *wh* words from the page and having the other person unscramble the word and write it correctly.

The letters *wh* stand for the beginning sounds in *what* and *who*.

Write the word from the box that rhymes with the numbered word. Then write *what* if the word you wrote has a *wh* that sounds like the *wh* in *what*. Write *who* if the word has a *wh* that sounds like the *wh* in *who*.

1. ten

_____

_____

2. try

_____

_____

3. lose

_____

_____

whip
whale
whole
when
where
why
whose
whim
whom
wheat

4. lip

_____

_____

5. mole

_____

_____

6. sale

_____

_____

7. loom

_____

_____

8. seat

_____

_____

9. pair

_____

_____

10. skim

_____

_____

Notes for Home: Your child wrote words with *wh*. **Home Activity:** Have your child name other rhyming words for the words in the box.

The prefixes *im-, dis-,* and *non-* can be added to the beginnings of words.

im + polite = impolite
dis + appear = disappear
non + living = nonliving

Find and circle a word with the prefix *im-, dis-,* or *non-* in each group of letters.

1. a d r i m p o s s i b l e r s

2. p r e n o n s t o p m e n t s

3. b e a b t e t d i s t r u s t

4. d i s a g r e e a g l e r e d

5. s o r i m p e r f e c t e t o n

Write the words you circled above to complete the sentences.

6. The cracked glass is _____.

7. I _____ with what you said.

8. The acrobat did a trick that looked _____ to do.

9. She is a person I _____.

10. The plane flies _____ to Dallas.

Notes for Home: Your child identified and wrote words with prefixes.
Home Activity: Take turns with your child making up a different sentence for each of the circled words.

The prefixes *im-*, *dis-*, and *non-* change the meaning but not the spelling of a word.

im + polite = impolite	not polite
dis + honest = dishonest	not honest
non + breakable = nonbreakable	not breakable

Add *im-*, *dis-,* or *non-* to make a new word. Then write the meaning of the new word.

1. _____ possible   _____

2. _____ loyal   _____

3. _____ stop   _____

4. _____ patient   _____

5. _____ trust   _____

6. _____ perfect   _____

7. _____ fiction   _____

8. _____ pleased   _____

9. _____ living   _____

10. _____ liked   _____

Notes for Home: Your child added prefixes to words and wrote meaning clues for the new words. **Home Activity:** Have your child look in newspapers and magazines for words with the prefixes *im-*, *dis-*, and *non-* and help him or her tell what each word means.

The vowels *a, e, i, o,* and *u* can stand for the vowel sound heard in unaccented syllables. This vowel sound is called the schwa sound. Listen for the schwa sound in these words.

about   tak**e**n   penc**i**l   mel**o**n   circ**u**s

Write the vowel that stands for the schwa sound in each word.

1. ago _____   **2.** kitchen _____   **3.** today _____

4. focus _____   **5.** cabin _____   **6.** number _____

7. major _____   **8.** allow _____   **9.** useful _____

10. dollar _____   **11.** fallen _____   **12.** actor _____

Match the beginning of each sentence to its ending. Write each sentence. Circle two words with the schwa sound.

I got two gallons of milk   as citrus fruit.

Lemons are known   tuna salad sandwich.

I made one tasty   at Al's grocery store.

13. _____

14. _____

15. _____

Notes for Home: Your child identified words with the schwa sound.
Home Activity: Have your child tell you how he or she thinks a favorite dish is prepared.
Listen for and call attention to words used that have the schwa sound.

The vowels *a, e, i, o,* and *u* can stand for the schwa sound. Listen for the schwa sound in these words.

about   tak**e**n   penc**i**l   lem**o**n   circ**u**s

Write the words in each box that have the schwa sound.

Animals		**Clothes**	
zebra	1. _____	shirt	4. _____
horse	2. _____	trousers	5. _____
otter	3. _____	sweater	6. _____
parakeet		slippers	

Number Words		**Buildings**	
seven	7. _____	skyscraper	10. _____
thirty	8. _____	cabin	11. _____
eleven	9. _____	apartment	12. _____
hundred		house	

Food	
apple	13. _____
banana	14. _____
bread	15. _____
chicken	

Notes for Home: Your child identified words with the schwa sound.
Home Activity: With your child, name other words that could be included in each category. Check to see if any of them have the schwa sound.

The letters *a, e, i, o,* and *u* stand for the schwa sound in these words.

about   tak**e**n   rob**i**n   lem**o**n   circ**u**s

Write the word for each picture. Then write the letter that stands for the schwa sound.

| sweater | apple | pencil | carrot | cactus |
| cabin | seven | zebra | walrus | wagon |

1.

_____ _____

2.

_____ _____

3.

_____ _____

4.

_____ _____

5.

_____ _____

6.

_____ _____

7.

_____ _____

8.

_____ _____

9.

_____ _____

10.

_____ _____

Notes for Home: Your child wrote words and the letters that stand for the schwa sound.
Home Activity: With your child, look in a magazine for pictures of things whose names have the schwa sound.

The letters *wh* stand for the beginning sounds in these words.

what   **wh**o

Put a check by each word in which *wh* stands for the same sound as in the word at the top of the box.

what		**who**	
1. white	_____	**11.** whom	_____
2. whale	_____	**12.** while	_____
3. wheel	_____	**13.** wharf	_____
4. when	_____	**14.** whoever	_____
5. whole	_____	**15.** which	_____
6. where	_____	**16.** wholesome	_____
7. whether	_____	**17.** why	_____
8. whose	_____	**18.** wholly	_____
9. whistle	_____	**19.** whip	_____
10. whirl	_____	**20.** wholesale	_____

Write a word you checked above to complete each sentence.

21. The kitten is black with _____ paws.

22. Wheat bread is often thought to be a _____ food.

23. To _____ is this gift to be sent?

24. The referee blew a _____ because of a foul.

25. A _____ is a large sea mammal.

Notes for Home: Your child identified words in *wh* stands for two different sounds.
Home Activity: Help your child choose five words from the boxes and put them in alphabetical order.

Name_____

The letters *wh* stand for two different sounds: the sound heard in *what* and the sound heard in *who*.

Circle the *wh* word or words in each question. Then answer the question. If you are not sure, make up your own answer.

1. Where did Little Miss Muffet sit?

_____

2. Who did Simple Simon meet?

_____

3. Whose mittens were lost?

_____

4. What followed Mary to school?

_____

5. Why did Jack and Jill go up a hill?

_____

6. Where was the cow while Little Boy Blue was asleep?

_____

7. By when was the cobbler to have the shoe mended?

_____

8. For whom did Old Mother Hubbard go to the cupboard?

_____

9. Which animal—the cow or the cat—jumped over the moon?

_____

10. Who wanted to see whether they could put Humpty Dumpty together again?

_____

Notes for Home: Your child wrote words with *wh*. **Home Activity:** Say some nursery rhymes with your child such as "Mary Had a Little Lamb" or "Little Miss Muffet." Point out any *wh* words you say.

To count the number of syllables in a word, count the number of vowel sounds you hear.

side	one vowel sound	=	one syllable
teacher	two vowel sounds	=	two syllables
uniform	three vowel sounds	=	three syllables

Look at and say the picture name. Write the number of vowels you **see** in the first box. Write the number of vowels you **hear** in the second box. Write the number of syllables in the word in the third box.

1. truck

2. chicken

3. penguin

4. peach

5. notebook

6. elephant

7. squirrel

8. butterfly

9. kangaroo

10. dinosaur

Notes for Home: Your child counted the number of syllables in words.
Home Activity: Take turns with your child naming an object in the room and telling how many syllables are in its name.

Sometimes dividing a word into parts can help you read a word you do not know.

- Divide between the two smaller words in a compound word.

    doghouse   dog/house

- Divide between a prefix, a suffix, or an ending and the base word.

    re/read   pay/ment   un/fold/ed   care/less/ness

Rewrite the words. Use slashes to show where to divide the words.

1. graceful _____

2. birthday _____

3. popcorn _____

4. softly _____

5. unlucky _____

6. inside _____

7. breakfast _____

8. weekend _____

9. maybe _____

10. unpack _____

11. bedroom _____

12. unsafe _____

13. airport _____

14. cheerful _____

15. distrustful _____

16. unkindness _____

17. unsafely _____

18. backyard _____

19. playfully _____

20. moonlight _____

Notes for Home: Your child divided compound words and words with affixes into syllables.
Home Activity: Help your child list some compound words and divide each word into syllables by drawing slashes between syllables.

Sometimes looking for small parts in a big word can help you read the word.

- • Look for affixes.   **un**/like/**ly**   **re**/place/**ment**
- • Look for little words you already know.   **out**/ward   **ten**/sion
- • Look for familiar vowel patterns.   mon/s**oo**n   pro/c**ee**d   re/b**a**te

Write the syllables of each word on the lines below. One syllable is already written for you.

independent	emergency	embarrassment
receptionist	spitefulness	reconstruction
neighborhood	convenience	establishment
photosynthesis	electromagnet	gymnastics
splendidly	prescription	unhappiness

1. _____ / _____ / ly

2. es / _____ / _____ / _____

3. _____ / _____ / _____ / the / _____

4. _____ / _____ / tics

5. _____ / _____ / pi / _____

6. _____ / _____ / _____ / ist

7. _____ / _____ / tro / _____ / _____

8. em / _____ / _____ / _____

9. _____ / _____ / struc / _____

10. _____ / ful / _____

11. _____ / _____ / i / _____

12. _____ / de / _____ / _____

13. _____ / scrip / _____

14. _____ / _____ / _____ / cy

15. _____ / bor / _____

Notes for Home: Your child divided words into syllables. **Home Activity:** Have your child look through a newspaper article and highlight words with three or more syllables.

When adding the ending *-ed* or *-ing,* the spelling of a word sometimes has to be changed.

start, start**ed**, start**ing**   no change
hope, hop**ed**, hop**ing**   drop the final *e*
stop, stop**ped**, stop**ping**   double the final consonant
try, tr**ied**   change *y* to *i*
try, try**ing**   no change

Add *-ed* or *-ing* to each word in the box to make a word that completes each sentence. Write the new word.

swim	fly	hurry	chase	laugh
hop	paint	move	cry	study

1. She _____ hard for the spelling test.

2. Let's go _____ in the pool to cool off.

3. Who _____ into the house next to yours?

4. The unhappy baby started _____ again.

5. In the movie, a kangaroo was _____ over a fence.

6. Our dog _____ the squirrel up the tree.

7. I like _____ pictures of dinosaurs with my watercolor set.

8. We saw some geese _____ south.

9. I _____ outside, so I would not miss the bus.

10. We were all _____ at the silly joke.

Notes for Home: Your child added the endings *-ed* and *-ing* to words, making spelling changes where needed. **Home Activity:** Take turns with your child telling about something you like to do. See how many *-ed* and *-ing* words you use.

Adding *-er* to some words can make them mean "more."
Add *-est* to some words can make them mean "most."

sad   sadd**er** (more sad)   sadd**est** (most sad)

Add *-er* or *-est* to make each word mean "more" or "most." Remember to make spelling changes if necessary.

1. most big

_____

2. more wide

_____

3. most dry

_____

4. more light

_____

5. most tall

_____

6. most large

_____

7. more heavy

_____

8. more old

_____

9. more tame

_____

10. more quick

_____

11. most flat

_____

12. most wet

_____

13. more brave

_____

14. most easy

_____

15. more muddy

_____

Notes for Home: Your child wrote words ending in *-er* and *-est*. **Home Activity:** Have your child list ten words that end with *-er* and ten words that end with *-est* and then use "more" and "most" to tell what each word means.

The letters *aw, au,* and *al* stand for the vowel sound in these words.

dr<u>aw</u>   **c<u>au</u>se**   **h<u>al</u>l**

Write the letters that stand for the vowel sound you hear in *draw* in each word.
Underline *beginning, middle,* or *end* to show where you hear that vowel sound.

1. raw   _____

   beginning   middle   end

2. talk   _____

   beginning   middle   end

3. small   _____

   beginning   middle   end

4. awesome   _____

   beginning   middle   end

5. lawn   _____

   beginning   middle   end

6. thaw   _____

   beginning   middle   end

7. paw   _____

   beginning   middle   end

8. salt   _____

   beginning   middle   end

9. stall   _____

   beginning   middle   end

10. falling   _____

   beginning   middle   end

11. sauce   _____

   beginning   middle   end

12. pause   _____

   beginning   middle   end

13. claws   _____

   beginning   middle   end

14. walk   _____

   beginning   middle   end

15. because   _____

   beginning   middle   end

Notes for Home: In this activity, your child identified the *aw, au,* and *al* vowel patterns in
words. **Home Activity:** Take turns with your child naming a word on the page and then
naming another word on the page with the same vowel sound and spelling.

Name_____

The same vowel sound can be spelled by different letter pairs.

dr**aw**　　　　　　c**au**se　　　　　　h**all**

Add the letters *aw, au,* or *al* to make the words in the list.

baseball　　draw　　author　　auto　　false
hawk　　　　fall　　chalk　　straw　　faucet

1. h ___ ___ k

2. dr ___ ___

3. f ___ ___ l

4. ___ ___ to

5. ch ___ ___ k

6. str ___ ___

7. baseb ___ ___ l

8. ___ ___ thor

9. f ___ ___ se

10. f ___ ___ cet

Write the word from above that goes with each clue.

11. Use this to write on the board.　　_____

12. A pitcher throws this.　　_____

13. This is a kind of bird.　　_____

14. This is another word for *car.*　　_____

15. Turn on water with this.　　_____

16. To make a picture, do this.　　_____

17. It is the opposite of *true.*　　_____

18. You can drink through this.　　_____

19. If you trip, you might do this.　　_____

20. This person writes books.　　_____

© Scott Foresman 3

Notes for Home: Your child identified and wrote words with the *aw, au,* and *al* vowel patterns. **Home Activity:** Both you and your child should draw a picture for one of the words on the page. Together tell a story to go with each picture.

Draw, cause, and *hall* all have the same vowel sound. But different letters stand for the vowel sound in each word.

Write the word that belongs in each group. Then write the letters that stand for the vowel sound you hear in *draw*.

auto	pause	August	chalk	autumn
baseball	walnut	small	draw	also
hawk	author	straw	auditorium	gnaw

1. little, tiny, _____   _____

2. bus, truck, _____   _____

3. paint, color, _____   _____

4. football, basketball, _____   _____

5. wait, rest, _____   _____

6. board, eraser, _____   _____

7. arena, theater, _____   _____

8. eagle, falcon, _____   _____

9. bite, chew, _____   _____

10. acorn, cashew, _____   _____

11. spring, summer, _____   _____

12. in addition, too, _____   _____

13. writer, poet, _____   _____

14. June, July, _____   _____

15. grass, hay, _____   _____

Notes for Home: Your child wrote words with the *aw, au,* and *al* vowel patterns.
Home Activity: Help your child make up other groups of three words and tell how the words go together.

Name _____

The vowels—*a, e, i, o, u*—can stand for a vowel sound called the schwa sound. You hear the schwa sound in unaccented syllables. Listen for the schwa sound in these words.

zebr**a**   sweat**e**r   penc**i**l   lem**o**n   circ**u**s

Write each word under the word that has the same spelling for the schwa sound.

grocery   tuna   eleven   carrot   citrus
awful   tractor   cabin   salad   focus
cabinet   vessel   stencil   allow   actor

      zebr**a**

      sweat**e**r
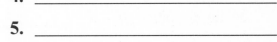

1. _____   4. _____

2. _____   5. _____

3. _____   6. _____

      penc**i**l

      lem**o**n

7. _____   10. _____

8. _____   11. _____

9. _____   12. _____

      circ**u**s

13. _____

14. _____

15. _____

Notes for Home: Your child sorted words according to the spelling of their schwa sound.
Home Activity: Help your child use a dictionary to find ten more words with the schwa sound. (The schwa symbol is /ə/ in a dictionary.)

Name_____

The vowels *a, e, i, o,* and *u* stand for the schwa sound in these words.

about   tak**e**n   penc**i**l   lem**o**n   circ**u**s

Complete each rhyme by writing a word from the list with the schwa sound. Circle the letter that stands for the schwa sound.

tractor	liver	ago	wagon	awful
cabinet	eleven	bacon	liner	slippers

1. Lots of white, fluffy snow

   Fell not too long _____.   a   e   i   o   u

2. There are tiny silver zippers

   On the fancy bedroom _____.   a   e   i   o   u

3. I ate only a tiny sliver

   Of the big piece of _____.   a   e   i   o   u

4. Dad used the Internet

   To buy a wooden _____.   a   e   i   o   u

5. In the movie the actor

   Had to drive a big green _____.   a   e   i   o   u

6. She just turned seven,

   But I am not _____.   a   e   i   o   u

7. There is nothing finer

   Than a trip on an ocean _____.   a   e   i   o   u

8. The gentle striped dragon

   Was pulling a _____.   a   e   i   o   u

9. So much gum all in one jawful

   Gave me a pain that was _____.   a   e   i   o   u

10. If I am not mistaken,

    That wonderful smell is _____.   a   e   i   o   u

Notes for Home: Your child wrote words with the schwa sound to complete rhymes.
Home Activity: Take turns with your child choosing another word with the schwa sound and making up a rhyme for the word.

The letters *ui* and *ew* stand for the vowel sound in these words

bru**ui**se   bl**ew**

Write the word from the box that means the same as the clue. Then circle the letters *ui* or *ew* that stand for the vowel sound.

newspaper	suit	crew	new	drew
juice	grew	cruise	fruit	chew

1. sail from place to place   _____

2. what someone did who is now taller   _____

3. apples, bananas, and grapes, for example   _____

4. never used   _____

5. liquid from an orange or other fruit   _____

6. jacket and pants that go together   _____

7. something to read that has today's information _____

8. people who work together as a team   _____

9. what someone did who sketched a picture   _____

10. what the dog did to a bone   _____

Notes for Home: Your child wrote words with the vowel patterns *ui* and *ew*.
Home Activity: Have your child choose some words from the box and use them to begin a story. Then take turns adding to the story.

In *suit,* the vowel sound is spelled *ui.* In *new,* the same vowel sound is spelled *ew.*

Follow the directions to make new words. Then circle the letters that stand for the vowel sound.

1. Start with **bruise.**
   Take away the **b.**
   Add **c.** Write the new word.

   _____

2. Start with **crew.**
   Take away the **cr.**
   Add **dr.** Write the new word.

   _____

3. Start with **fruit.**
   Take away the **fr.**
   Add **s.** Write the new word.

   _____

4. Start with **blew.**
   Take away the **bl.**
   Add **ch.** Write the new word.

   _____

5. Start with **flew.**
   Take away the **fl.**
   Add **gr.** Write the new word.

   _____

6. Start with **judo.**
   Take away the **do.**
   Add **ice.** Write the new word.

   _____

7. Start with **grew.**
   Take away the **gr.**
   Add **bl.** Write the new word.

   _____

8. Start with **drew.**
   Take away the **d.**
   Add **c.** Write the new word.

   _____

9. Start with **suit.**
   Take away the **s.**
   Add **fr.** Write the new word.

   _____

10. Start with **cruise.**
    Take away the **cr.**
    Add **br.** Write the new word.

    _____

Notes for Home: Your child wrote words with the vowel patterns *ui* and *ew.*
Home Activity: Have your child use two of the *ui* or *ew* words from the page to write a rhyme.

Name _____

The letters *ui* and *ew* stand for the vowel sound in *bruise* and *chew*.

Write the word from the box that completes each phrase. Circle the letters that stand for a vowel sound.

juice	drew	suit	grew	flew
new	fruit	crew	cruise	blew

1. rode my brand-_____ bike   ui   ew

2. _____ a picture of our cat   ui   ew

3. drank some fresh orange _____   ui   ew

4. ate a banana from a bowl of _____   ui   ew

5. the _____ of the space shuttle   ui   ew

6. geese that _____ over our house   ui   ew

7. jacket for a business _____   ui   ew

8. winds that _____ 40 miles per hour   ui   ew

9. _____ vegetables to eat   ui   ew

10. take a _____ to Bermuda   ui   ew

Notes for Home: Your child wrote words with the *ui* and *ew* vowel patterns.
Home Activity: Take turns with your child making up new phrases or sentences for each word in the box.

Dividing words into syllables may help you read words you do not know.

- To count the number of syllables in a word, count the number of vowel sounds.
- Divide between the two smaller words in a compound word.

  doghouse   dog/house

- Divide between a prefix, a suffix, or an ending and the base word.

  re/read   go/ing   dis/place/ment   care/less/ness

Write each word under the heading that tells how many syllables it has. Then draw lines to show how to divide each word into syllables.

repayment	distrustful	unkindness	outside	unsafely
crying	unfairness	homework	leadership	playground
sunglasses	displeased	careless	replace	rebuilding
doing	crewmate	mistreatment	playfully	meanwhile

Two-Syllable Words

1. _____   2. _____

3. _____   4. _____

5. _____   6. _____

7. _____   8. _____

9. _____   10. _____

Three-Syllable Words

11. _____   12. _____

13. _____   14. _____

15. _____   16. _____

17. _____   18. _____

19. _____   20. _____

Notes for Home: Your child sorted two- and three-syllable words and divided the words into syllables. **Home Activity:** Have your child find some two- and three-syllable words in a newspaper or magazine.

Name_____

Sometimes looking for small parts in a big word can help you read the word.

- Look for affixes. **un**/like/**ly**   **re**/place/**ment**
- Look for little words you already know. **out**/ward   **ten**/sion
- Look for familiar vowel patterns. mon/s**oo**n   pro/c**ee**d   re/b**a**te

Match each word with a clue. Write the word in syllables.

unhealthy	subtraction	Tennessee	illustrate	imprison
skeleton	televise	reminder	basketball	endlessly
chimpanzee	yesterday	promotion	Washington	pantomime

1. a southern state   _____ / _____ / _____

2. never stopping   _____ / _____ / _____

3. 25 − 11 = 13   _____ / _____ / _____

4. gestures without words   _____ / _____ / _____

5. broadcast on TV   _____ / _____ / _____

6. movement to a higher level   _____ / _____ / _____

7. small ape   _____ / _____ / _____

8. game played with a large, round ball   _____ / _____ / _____

9. all the bones in the body   _____ / _____ / _____

10. not well   _____ / _____ / _____

11. make pictures for   _____ / _____ / _____

12. the day before today   _____ / _____ / _____

13. put in prison   _____ / _____ / _____

14. something to help you remember   _____ / _____ / _____

15. first U.S. president   _____ / _____ / _____

Notes for Home: Your child divided words into syllables. **Home Activity:** Take turns with your child finding a long word in a story and dividing it into syllables. Be sure to check your answers in a dictionary.

When an affix is added to a word, a spelling change may or may not be needed.

- **Prefixes**
  no spelling change   happy   **un**happy
- **Suffixes and Endings**
  no spelling change   go   go**ing**
  drop the final *e*   hope   hop**ing**
  double the final consonant   big   big**ger**
  change *y* to *i*   happy   happ**iness**

Add the affix or affixes shown. Write the new word.

1. The dinner tasted (wonder + ful).   _____

2. I could hardly wait to (un + wrap) the gift.   _____

3. She sang (happy + ly) all morning.   _____

4. The kitchen faucet is (drip + ing).   _____

5. The (smile + ing) baby laughed.   _____

6. I (like + ed) the movie.   _____

7. Where is the (swim + ing) pool?   _____

8. The sun was shining (bright + ly).   _____

9. They were (dis + please + ed) with the work.   _____

10. She slept (un + easy + ly) through the storm.   _____

Notes for Home: Your child added affixes—prefixes, suffixes, and endings—to words.
Home Activity: Together with your child choose one of the sentences and use it to begin a
story. Try to use words with affixes as you tell the story.

Name _____

A word may have one or more affixes added to it.

Prefix	**Suffix**	**Ending**	**More Than One Affix**
disappear	appear**ance**	appear**ing**	**dis**appear**ance**

Write each word to show what affixes were added.

sickness	unhappy	incorrectly	unpacking	repainted
drawing	shortest	distrusted	impolitely	sadly

Prefix	**Base Word**	**Suffix or Ending**

1. _____   _____   _____

2. _____   _____   _____

3. _____   _____   _____

4. _____   _____   _____

5. _____   _____   _____

6. _____   _____   _____

7. _____   _____   _____

8. _____   _____   _____

9. _____   _____   _____

10. _____   _____   _____

© Scott Foresman 3

Notes for Home: Your child identified affixes—prefixes, suffixes, and endings—in words.
Home Activity: Together with your child look through a favorite book for words with affixes.
Take turns naming the base word and the affixes added.

Name _____

When affixes are added to words, a spelling change may be needed.

Underline the word in the sentence that has an affix or affixes added. Then write the base word and the affixes.

1. I disagree with your idea.

Base Word _____   Affix or Affixes _____

2. That is the biggest snake I have ever seen.

Base Word _____   Affix or Affixes _____

3. They cried when they heard the sad story.

Base Word _____   Affix or Affixes _____

4. I like a movie that is humorous.

Base Word _____   Affix or Affixes _____

5. She is hoping to go to the park.

Base Word _____   Affix or Affixes _____

6. Our team was victorious.

Base Word _____   Affix or Affixes _____

7. Who uncovered the treasure chest?

Base Word _____   Affix or Affixes _____

8. Why are you displeased with the book?

Base Word _____   Affix or Affixes _____

9. The huge rock is immovable.

Base Word _____   Affix or Affixes _____

10. We sat impatiently because the play did not begin on time.

Base Word _____   Affix or Affixes _____

Notes for Home: Your child identified base words and affixes—prefixes, suffixes, and endings. **Home Activity:** Together with your child look through junk mail for examples of words with affixes. Tell what the base word is and what affixes were added.

The letters *aw, au,* and *al* stand for the vowel sound in these words.

dr**aw**   **cau**se   h**all**

Draw lines to match two rhyming words with the same spelling for the vowel sound.

1. call	talk		**6.** claw	dawn
2. walk	law		**7.** salt	halt
3. lawn	wall		**8.** haul	waltz
4. cause	drawn		**9.** false	flaw
5. paw	pause		**10.** yawn	Paul

Write each pair of words you matched above. Write the letters that stand for the vowel sound.

Words   **Vowel Sound**

11. _____ and _____   _____

12. _____ and _____   _____

13. _____ and _____   _____

14. _____ and _____   _____

15. _____ and _____   _____

16. _____ and _____   _____

17. _____ and _____   _____

18. _____ and _____   _____

19. _____ and _____   _____

20. _____ and _____   _____

Notes for Home: Your child matched rhyming words with *aw, au,* and *al*.
Home Activity: Together with your child use pairs of words from the page to make up silly rhymes.

The letters *aw, au,* and *al* stand for the vowel sound in *draw, cause,* and *hall.*

Write the word that answers the question. Circle the letters that stand for the vowel sound you hear in *draw.*

1. Can chalk or yawns squeak? _____

2. Does a snake crawl or walk? _____

3. Could a person drive a straw or an auto? _____

4. Does the lawn or the hall get mowed? _____

5. Would you call or draw a picture? _____

6. Can an author or an altar write a book? _____

7. Is a skyscraper tall or small? _____

8. Would you eat a scrawl or a walnut? _____

9. Is a horse kept in a crawl or a stall? _____

10. Would you cook sauce or chalk? _____

11. Do claws or hawks fly? _____

12. Would you hit a flaw or a baseball? _____

13. Do you wash laundry or lawyers? _____

14. Would you turn on a faucet or a pause? _____

15. Would you sit in an auditorium or a drawer? _____

Notes for Home: Your child wrote words with the vowel patterns *aw, au,* and *al.*
Home Activity: Take turns with your child choosing a word that was not an answer on the page and asking a question about the word.